Managing Editor: Rick Joyner
Contributing Editors: Jack Deere, Francis Frangipane, Dudley Hall
Assistant Editor: Deborah Joyner Johnson
Project Manager: Dana Zondory
Layout and Design: Dana Zondory
Copy Editors: Roger Hedgspeth, Suzanne Hirt, and Deborah Williams

The Morning Star Journal® USPS012-903 is published quarterly, 4 issues per year, by MorningStar Publications, Inc., a division of MorningStar Fellowship Church, 375 Star Light Drive, Fort Mill, SC 29715. Fall 2006 issue. Periodicals postage rates paid at Wilkesboro, NC and additional mailing offices. CPC Agreement #1472593. ISSN# 10832122

POSTMASTER: Send address corrections to *The Morning Star Journal*®, 375 Star Light Drive, Fort Mill, SC 29715

Subscription rates: One year $17.50; Outside U.S. $24.95 USD.

MorningStar Publications is a non-profit organization dedicated to the promulgation of important teachings and timely prophetic messages to the church. We also attempt to promote interchange between the different streams and denominations in the body of Christ.

To receive a subscription to *The Morning Star Journal*®, send payment along with your name and address to *MorningStar Publications*, 375 Star Light Drive, Fort Mill, SC 29715, (803) 802-5544 (1-800-542-0278—Credit Card Orders Only); fax (704) 285-7251. One year (4 quarterly issues) U.S. $17.50; Outside U.S. $24.95 USD. Prices are subject to change without notice.

Reprints—Photocopies of any part of the contents of this publication may be made freely. However, to re-typeset information, permission must be requested in writing from *MorningStar Publications Department*, 375 Star Light Drive, Fort Mill, SC 29715

THE MORNING STAR JOURNAL
VOLUME 17—LIFE IN THE SPIRIT

NO. 1—THE HOLY SPIRIT

STRONG FOUNDATIONS

THE OVERCOMING LIFE

THE GREAT SOCIETY

WORLD CHANGERS

PROPHETIC PERSPECTIVES

Y0-AFV-092

STRONG FOUNDATIONS

Growing Stronger, Deeper Roots in Sound Biblical Truth

Earnestly Desire the Spiritual

by Rick Joyner

The Christian circles who believe the gifts of the Holy Spirit are no longer operational in the church often cite how the Corinthian church, which had all of the gifts operating, were called **"still carnal" (see I Corinthians 2:3 NKJV)** by Paul, as if the gifts of the Spirit were the cause of this carnality. If the gifts of the Holy Spirit were the cause of their carnality, why would the apostle actually encourage them to seek the gifts even more, which he did in his letters to them?

When Paul chastised the Corinthians for being **"carnal,"** this word could have been translated "natural." He was chastising them for not being spiritual enough. Paul was actually being a little more radical in encouraging the Corinthians to pursue the spiritual than some modern English translations imply. Let's look at a couple of verses to see how:

> **Now concerning spiritual *gifts*, brethren, I do not want you to be unaware (I Corinthians 12:1).**

> **Pursue love, yet desire earnestly spiritual *gifts*... (I Corinthians 14:1).**

In the verses above, the word **"gifts"** is italicized because it is not found in the original manuscripts. It was added because the translators assumed that the gifts were what Paul was implying. This may be the case, but not necessarily. Since the word **"gifts"** is not there, let us consider how these verses literally read, adding only the word "the" before "**spiritual**" as good English grammar would require:

> **Now concerning the spiritual, brethren, I do not want you to be unaware (I Corinthians 12:1).**

> **Pursue love, yet desire earnestly the spiritual... (I Corinthians 14:1).**

My point here is that adding the word "**gifts**" to these verses actually reduces and limits the scope of what was said. Spiritual gifts are included in the awareness of the spiritual, which we should have and should be pursuing, but the spiritual gifts are not all which we should be aware of and pursue. We should in fact pursue the spiritual realm. What exactly does this mean?

The spiritual realm is more real, or has more substance, than the natural realm.

It will take more than one article to answer this question, but to answer it is essential for Christianity in the twenty-first century. The emerging generation will not settle for a faith based solely on the works of God in history, but they will have to see and experience them in their own lives. True, biblical Christianity is the most exciting adventure that one can experience in this life. Nothing is more boring than mere religion, and that which is not based on a living faith will not survive long in these times.

The spiritual realm is more real, or has more substance, than the natural realm. God is Spirit. That which takes place in the spiritual realm can impact the natural realm far more than what takes place in the natural realm. The beings who dwell in the spiritual realm, such as angels and demons, have the authority to extraordinarily impact the physical. Physically, we can do nothing in the spiritual realm, but by faith, which is spiritual, we can do much. The spiritual trumps the natural in every way. For this reason, one basic aspect of true Christian maturity is to be more at home in the spiritual realm than in the natural, just as the Apostle Paul stated in II Corinthians 5:6-8:

Therefore, being always of good courage, and knowing that while we are at home in the body we are absent from the Lord—

for we walk by faith, not by sight—

we are of good courage, I say, and prefer rather to be absent from the body and to be at home with the Lord.

As a great saint of old once stated, the new creation man is not called to be a human being who has occasional spiritual experiences, but we are called to be spiritual beings who have occasional human experiences.

We should be more at home in the spiritual realm than we are in the natural. We should actually, as Paul also stated in II Corinthians 5, literally be groaning for our spiritual bodies wanting to be free of the natural.

We cannot truly fight the battle between light and darkness without understanding the spiritual realm to at least some degree.

Those who are led by fear instead of faith will often quickly and automatically reject what they cannot understand or cannot control. Such will point to the cults and New Age movements as evidence that the supernatural realm belongs to the devil. These have more faith in the devil to deceive them than they do in the Holy Spirit to lead them to the truth. The devil would very much like to totally possess and control the high ground of the spiritual realm. However, as the Scripture makes clear in II Corinthians 10:4: **"For the weapons of our warfare are not carnal** (or natural), **but mighty in God for pulling down strongholds" (NKJV).** We cannot truly fight the battle between light and darkness without understanding the spiritual realm to at least some degree, along with the spiritual nature of the weapons we have been given to fight within this realm.

SEEK TO FIND

Even so, the Holy Spirit will not impose Himself or experiences on those who do not want them. That is why Paul encouraged the Corinthians to seek the spiritual, because if we do not seek it we will not receive it. Those who say that they are "open" for the Lord to do anything He wants with them do not understand a basic principle of the kingdom—we have to seek in order to find. We have to care about something enough to seek it before He will entrust it to us. That's why those who are "open" to be used in spiritual gifts are never used. We have to honor them more than this to receive them.

One of the most notable and worn-out sayings is, "You can become so spiritually-minded that you are no longer any earthly good." The truth is that most Christians have been so earthly-minded that they have not done any good in heaven or the earth. By having spiritual authority, we can do far more in even the natural realm than we could otherwise. The church which becomes what it is called to be will be so heavenly-minded she will not care very much for the carnal, temporary things of this world, and because of that, she will be used to have the greatest impact for good on this world.

Kids are looking to the supernatural for power and they cannot find it in the church.

It is time to earnestly desire the spiritual. The great battle between light and darkness at the end of this age will become increasingly spiritual and increasingly supernatural. Through movies, books, and other forms of entertainment, the emerging generation is becoming increasingly drawn into the spiritual and supernatural. This is why cults and covens are growing so fast—the kids are looking to the supernatural for power and they cannot find it in the church. This will and is even now changing, but we must go beyond just having doctrines in which we believe the supernatural power of God is available to actually having it. Normal Christianity is supernatural.

Seeing angels is normal Christianity. In the first century, this was obviously a very common experience, as angels released Peter from prison. When he came to the door to get into the house where they were praying for him, it was easier for them to believe it was his angel at the door than Peter (see Acts 12:7-11). The Book of Acts contains a number of other encounters between angels and believers. We should not think this is strange since they are **"ministering spirits" (see Hebrews 1:14)** called to serve those who are the heirs of salvation.

When we start to see angels, it is not because they are entering our realm as much as we are beginning to enter their realm. We begin to see into the spiritual realm when the "eyes of our hearts" start to open. When Elisha sat on the side of the hill unconcerned about the entire army which was coming after him, it was because he could see that those who were with him, the angels, far outnumbered those who were coming after him. His servant could not see this, so Elisha prayed for his eyes to be opened (see II Kings 6).

FIGHT THE GOOD FIGHT

Then Elisha called on their power to strike the enemy with blindness, which did happen, and he was able to capture an entire army. I think that was greater than what even the greatest commando could have done! We, too, must begin to see into the spiritual realm—make it our home more than this earthly realm and learn to use the "divinely powerful weapons" we have been given to fight with.

The Corinthians were chastised for being carnal because of the divisions among them. The reason for many of our divisions is that we are too occupied with the natural, earthly things which are really not that significant. If we start to see from God's perspective, the heavenly one, we will not be nearly as prone to divide over the things that now upset us and cause conflicts between us. If we could see from the heavenly perspective, we would not waste nearly as much energy fighting with our fellow believers and focus on fighting our true enemy. Even then, we would not be overly concerned about the enemy either, knowing that He who is with us is much greater than he who is against us.

JESUS IS THE DOOR

Our main purpose for entering the spiritual realm and making it our home is more than just fighting. God is Spirit, and for us to know Him as He is we must perceive Him as He is and worship Him in spirit and truth (see John 4:23). Our goal is not just to be spiritual, but to be one with the Lord, to abide in Him and be filled with His Spirit. There is nothing higher than abiding in Christ. He is seated at the right hand of the Father, above all rule and authority and dominion. To be seated with Him in the heavenly places is not only our calling; it is the ultimate position that can be attained in all of creation.

It is the Lord's desire to use us, as members of His body, as extensions of His authority and power, to do as He did—to go about doing good and destroying the works of the devil. The way that Jesus preached the kingdom was to demonstrate its authority over any conditions that were on the earth, including disease, afflictions, or any need. In heaven, there are no cripples, so He demonstrated how touching a cripple with the authority of heaven would heal them. In heaven, there is no need, so He demonstrated how touching even just one little boy's lunch with the authority of heaven would multiply it until it fed thousands. In heaven, there is no death, so when the authority of heaven was used to touch the dead they would come back to life.

There is nothing higher than abiding in Christ.

When Jesus told Nathanael that He saw him under the fig tree and Nathanael responded with, **"Rabbi, You are the Son of God,"** the Lord answered him with, **"Because I said to you that I saw you under the fig tree, do you believe? You shall see greater things than these.... Truly, truly, I say to you, you shall see the heavens opened, and the angels of God ascending and descending on the Son of Man" (John 1:49-51).** Angels are His messengers, and it is the purpose of His messengers to ascend into heaven and bring back to the earth evidence of heaven's reality and its authority over any condition on the earth.

As the Scripture makes clear, **"For the kingdom of God does not consist in words, but in power" (I Corinthians 4:20).** The kingdom of God is coming to the earth, and before it does, the good news that it is coming will be preached throughout the whole world, but not just with words. The Lord Himself preached the gospel of the kingdom by demonstrating its authority over the earth and that is how the gospel of the kingdom will be preached.

It is time to seek the power of the Lord in our own lives. We need to seek it for the right reasons, and we need to be careful to use it in obedience to the Lord, but we must have power to be witnesses of the Almighty. This is not just power over conditions, but the power to transform those who are in even the worst bondage to a life that is more free and more glorious than can ever be attained apart from the New Covenant that we now have with God Almighty. In the time to come, the difference between being citizens of this world and being citizens of the kingdom will be revealed to the whole world. ■

Rick Joyner is the founder, executive director, and senior pastor of MorningStar Fellowship Church. Rick is a well-known author of more than forty books, including his most recent, *The Overcoming Life*. He also oversees MorningStar's School of Ministry, Fellowship of Ministries, and Fellowship of Churches. Rick and his wife, Julie, live in South Carolina and have five children: Anna, Aaryn, Amber, Ben, and Sam.

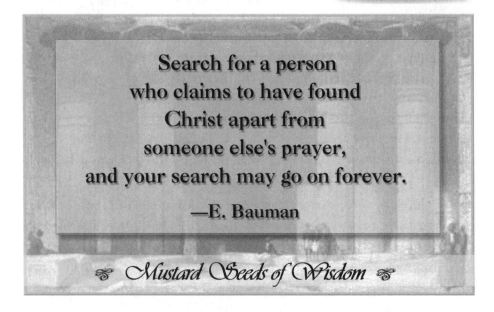

Search for a person
who claims to have found
Christ apart from
someone else's prayer,
and your search may go on forever.

—E. Bauman

❧ *Mustard Seeds of Wisdom* ❧

The Age of Advantage
by Dudley Hall

All Scriptures are English Standard Version.

Everyone in the delivery room seemed excited about a new life coming into the world. Everyone that is except one: the baby. He was evidently not too excited about changing environments. He had been very comfortable there for nine months, and the unknown prospects of living outside mother's womb were not too inviting. Mom was pushing. Nurses were pulling. Dad was coaching. Finally, the baby emerged crying and kicking.

Likewise, the disciples of Jesus had been with Him for three years. They had finally become somewhat comfortable with following Him. It had been a true challenge with many bumps, but now they were impressed with superiority over other teachers. They had seen the dead arise, the lame walk, the blind see, the hungry fed, the storms recede, and sins forgiven. Now, Jesus was telling them that He was leaving. A new era had arrived. The goal of history was at hand. They were privileged to live at the transition from the old era to the new. It would be to their advantage that He left.

THE COMING OF THE HOLY SPIRIT

At the beginning of history, God created mankind to enjoy fellowship with Him and to engage in partnership with Him. Adam and Eve would find true intimacy and purpose as they lived in this relationship. But, they chose to do it another way, and the whole of creation was affected by their sinful choice. However, God's purpose was not thwarted. He revealed Himself to Abram and promised that through his seed, God would redeem creation from the curse of the Fall. For hundreds of years, God prepared for that time. He used the physical descendants of Abraham as a shadow of the ultimate people who would again enjoy full fellowship and partnership with God on the earth. He gave them the Law as a guide, foreshadowing the ultimate Guide who would live inside them. He gave a temple as a type of the constant presence of God among His people. He gave them land as a picture of the ultimate inheritance they would receive as God's sons. He gave them a king to point toward the ultimate King who would reign over all for their benefit. Finally, He gave His Son as the Seed who would bring the shadows to substance and open the door to the new era. The disciples had been with the Son/Seed for some time, and now it was time for the transition. It would include His death, His resurrection, His ascension, and then the coming of the Holy Spirit.

"Nevertheless, I tell you the truth: it is to your advantage that I go away, for if I do not go away, the Helper will not come to you. But if I go, I will send him to you" (John 16:7).

What would be so advantageous for the disciples and for us? He makes it clear that the coming of the Holy Spirit would make the original mission possible. He alone would be able to convict the world of sin, righteousness, and judgment. Jesus had come to bear the sins of any man. There is no sin beyond His redemptive love. Those who reject the remedy have committed the sin for which there is no forgiveness. For all who have ever lived, the issue is not what caused our sin or the fairness of environment or parentage. Whatever may have influenced our lives, Jesus provided the solution and the issue of sin is one of faith or unbelief.

> The judgment of God is revealed in the exaltation of Jesus.

ADVANTAGES OF THE HOLY SPIRIT

The righteousness that every man inevitably craves is only available in Jesus. He alone can model it and perform it. He alone has pleased the Father and paid the penalty of unrighteousness. And the Holy Spirit alone can convince the human heart of this. He makes the work of Jesus real in the heart of the believer.

The judgment of God is revealed in the exaltation of Jesus. He drew the lines in history. He so completely revealed truth that all who receive Him are in the truth and all who reject Him are outside of truth. His death forever sealed the judgment of God on the deceiver and his followers. Only the Holy Spirit can make that judgment real. He alone can convince the heart of the ultimate justice in Jesus' death.

Another advantage of the new era of the Holy Spirit is the guarantee of full transfer of the inheritance. His mission is to take the meaning of Jesus' work and make it experiential for the spiritual seed of Abraham. He unlocks the divine reality.

"When the Spirit of truth comes, he will guide you into all the truth, for he will not speak on his own authority, but whatever he hears he will speak, and he will declare to you the things that are to come" (John 16:13).

The truth is more than just the facts. It is the purpose and meaning behind them. It is the living reality of eternal life expressing itself in love. He is the personal guide. He does not just show you the library filled with millions of books. He guides you into the vital truths that make life meaningful. Since we are each at a different point in the journey, we need more than a general curriculum. The Holy Spirit is our personal guide in the discovery of the treasure granted to us by grace.

He also unfolds the pertinent future. It will not be for the purpose of satisfying curiosity, but for meaningful participation in the purpose of God's plan—what we need to know for getting our assignment done. Our problems with predicting the future usually come from speculations of the curious mind mixed with the compulsion to be in control through superior knowledge. We tend to think that if we can know that which others don't, we can be prepared for whatever might happen. God seems to enjoy our dependence on Him as the mover and controller of world events.

Mostly, He unpacks the Son's inheritance.

"He will glorify me, for he will take what is mine and declare it to you" (John 16:14).

For instance, He fulfills the promises of the New Covenant.

"For this is the covenant that I will make with the house of Israel after those days, declares the Lord: I will put my laws

into their minds, and write them on their hearts, and I will be their God, and they shall be my people.

"And they shall not teach, each one his neighbor and each one his brother, saying, 'Know the Lord,' for they shall all know me, from the least of them to the greatest.

"For I will be merciful toward their iniquities, and I will remember their sins no more" (Hebrews 8:10-12).

The work of the Holy Spirit puts the law of God in our heads and hearts. He gives us both knowledge and desire. He alone can make forgiveness a reality in the midst of condemnation and a soiled conscience.

> Only the kind of love Jesus displayed can ever win the conflict between good and evil.

He fulfills Jesus' promise to never leave us alone.

"I will not leave you as orphans; I will come to you" (John 14:18).

The temple had represented a God who wanted to be with His people. Now in this advantageous age the people themselves would be the temple. Through the person of the Holy Spirit, each believer would know God personally, and the community of faith would know Him in His many-membered body. God would be "real" to them, but the world outside would not know Him.

He empowers believers to overcome evil through the supernatural power of unconditional love.

"This is my commandment, that you love one another as I have loved you" (John 15:12).

Force can never obliterate evil. Only the kind of love Jesus displayed can ever win the conflict between good and evil. He has impregnated His people with the power to love without ever getting any in return. The Holy Spirit has come inside to love through our faith. Love cannot be killed by the sword or erased by time. It is the life of God shared with His people. It will win.

He endues us with the privilege of fellowship and the dignity of partnership. Now we can live in His fellowship all the time, and we are assured that all our work has dignity since we are working in partnership with Him. Whether we work at the church house or in the cornfield, we are His representatives bringing the kingdom of heaven to earth.

How are we to embrace this age of advantage? There are several phrases referring to the relationship we have with the Holy Spirit. For instance, we are commanded to be filled with the Spirit. Actually the Apostle Paul compares this with being intoxicated with wine. The Spirit's influence on our perspective and behavior is noticeable. In the Book of Acts, believers are filled with the Spirit on different occasions with the noticeable results of boldness in speech and conduct as they fulfill their present assignments.

We are also baptized with/by the Spirit. "Baptize" usually reflects identification with someone. The children of Israel were baptized into Moses. In other words, he represented them to God, and they received whatever he received from God. When we are baptized into the name of Jesus we identify with Him. We are viewed by God the Father as "in Christ." It is the Holy Spirit who baptizes us into the name of Christ. To be baptized in the Spirit is to be identified with the age of the Spirit. It is to acknowledge that the time of the Old Covenant has been fulfilled, and that we have the privilege and responsibility to live by the power and guidance of the Spirit.

> We are assured that all our work has dignity since we are working in partnership with Him.

We are "Spirit people" in the best sense of that phrase. We are recipients of the inheritance of Jesus which is made real by the Spirit. As we walk the journey of faith, we have the wonderful experience of the Holy Spirit unpacking another aspect of the inheritance. Sadly, some try to camp there and make that "baptism" the qualifying experience for fellowship. Sometimes we do not know we need some things that are already ours by virtue of our being in Christ until confronted with a task beyond our present abilities. In desperation, we cry out for help. The answer is the

Holy Spirit's revelation of power and authority we need for the task. These gifts from the Spirit enable us to fulfill our mission of subduing the earth in fellowship with God.

We are also exhorted to walk in the Spirit. The context of this expression is the life of love made possible through the life of the Spirit. Walking in love is walking in the Spirit. He guides and empowers us to relate to each kind of person we will meet. We can by His strength live beyond our selfishness. We can enjoy the life of giving and serving.

We also have the privilege to be anointed by the Spirit. In the history of Israel, people were anointed with oil for specific callings. Priests were anointed as were kings. The anointing marks one for special assignment and grants them the authority and power to accomplish it. Since we are in the Anointed One, we have an anointing as His special people. In our specific callings and assignments, we can have an anointing that fits. God never gives us a job without the tools necessary to do it.

God never gives us a job without the tools necessary to do it.

SINS AGAINST THE SPIRIT

The Scripture mentions some sins against the Spirit. Knowing the nature of these can help us to understand the seriousness of living in the age of advantage.

Blasphemy is a scary word. Nothing good is said about the act of blasphemy. It is an act of bold and unmitigated disdain. To blaspheme against the Holy Spirit is to so shut your heart, so no matter what He did you would not recognize it as being from God. The Jews were quick to accuse Jesus of blasphemy because He would not fit their mold. They had concluded that He was not their Messiah. No matter what benevolent or miraculous work Jesus did in their midst, they ascribed its source to the devil, not to God.

One good thing to note is that if one is concerned that he/she has committed that sin, they haven't. That kind of hardness would not recognize its offense.

We can grieve the Spirit. Grieve is a love word. When we refuse to embrace love as the central feature of life, we grieve the Spirit. Acts of selfishness and self-protection are an offense to the Spirit of love. He always gives when given the choice.

Quenching the Spirit is mentioned in relationship to the various gifts of the Spirit. When we neglect or abuse His gifts, we put out the fire of His presence. Gifts can be messy, especially in the hands of immature believers, but if we are to express a supernatural kingdom to this world, we must have the various gifts of the Spirit operating.

We do live in the age of advantage. We are the people upon whom the climax of history has fallen. We have been redeemed by the shed blood of our Lord. We are indwelt by the Spirit of life. He has sealed us as the people of God. He has given us the spirit of adoption as God's children. We have been gifted with power and authority to bring the kingdom of God to earth as it is in heaven. The powers of hell have sought to keep believers ignorant of the advantage. Those who are have neglected a great salvation. Another tactic is to create fear of the Spirit life. Those who are fearful reject the very Person who came to give them the joy of fellowship with God and the dignity of partnership with Him. Those who embrace the person of the Holy Spirit in His fullness will find intimacy with God and meaning in life. ■

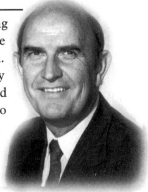

Dudley Hall is president of Successful Christian Living Ministries, a ministry dedicated to the restoration of the individual and the church according to God's original plan. As a teacher and popular conference speaker within the body of Christ, Dudley shares the truths which God has imparted to him simply and concisely, offering practical insights to enable believers to grow in their relationships with Christ. Dudley is the author of numerous books, which titles include *Grace Works*, *A Treasure Worth the Effort*, and *Incense and Thunder*. He and his wife, Betsy, live in Texas with their two children: David and Karis.

The Spirit of Truth

by Robin McMillan

All Scriptures are New King James Version unless otherwise noted.

In the early 1970s, I worked with a food service equipment company that outfitted commercial cooking establishments with a wide range of items, from teaspoons to walk-in refrigerators and freezers. One of our major accounts, a large national chain of drugstores, had over one hundred snack bars in the southeastern United States. Another young man and I received orders from them over the phone like: "Robin, send three dozen teaspoons to store #75 in Tuscaloosa, Alabama." I quickly grew bored with that part of my job and reluctantly handled my share of those orders.

John Mandanis, a gregarious Greek manager with that drugstore company, placed many of those orders. On one occasion, he phoned in an order for several dozen forks to be sent to one of his locations. A few days later, he came by the store to pick up some other things and asked if I had sent the forks yet. I quickly told him he must have placed the order with Gary, the other young man who handled orders. I shocked myself at how easily I lied over something so small. John scratched his head and wandered over to Gary's desk to talk to him about the order.

Instantly, the Holy Spirit convicted me. I knew that if I did not own up to what I had done that my dishonesty would lead to much more serious consequences down the road. My pride was all that stood between me and obedience to the Holy Spirit. I humbly called John aside and admitted that I had lied to him. Instead of condemning me, John smiled and said, "I expect better from you. Don't do that again." In a very practical and somewhat painful way, I learned the value that the Holy Spirit places on the truth. He wanted me to be honest with people in all of my dealings, both small and large.

I also saw the power that the truth released. Instead of losing my relationship with John Mandanis, I gained him as a friend. He knew I had not told him the truth in the beginning, but when I was willing to be honest with him, he realized he could trust me.

ANOTHER TEST

My love for the truth was tested over and over again in the business world. Once one of my bosses overheard a phone conversation I had with a customer who insisted I give him several hundred dollars our company owed him. My boss knew of the situation and realized that if I lied about the details of the transaction, I could save our company the money. "Lie to him! Lie to him!" he whispered to me as I spoke with the man on the phone. I was not going to lie to the man, even for my boss. In an instant the Holy Spirit gave me a word of wisdom. I put the customer on hold and said to my boss, "If I will lie *for* you, I will lie *to* you. What do you want me to do?"

He could not answer. He knew I was right. I returned to the phone and told the man we would send him a check that afternoon. My boss never asked me to lie for him again, nor did he ever mention that episode. He also learned through this that he could trust me with his business.

THE SPIRIT OF TRUTH

Jesus taught that the key to being free is in knowing the truth.

"And you shall know the truth, and the truth shall make you free" (John 8:32).

The Holy Spirit is the Spirit of Truth. He will guide us into truth if we listen and yield to Him.

"However, when He, the Spirit of truth, has come, He will guide you into all truth; for He will not speak on His own authority, but whatever He hears He will speak; and He will tell you things to come" (John 16:13).

KEY TO PERSONAL TRANSFORMATION

Jesus once ministered to a Samaritan woman at Jacob's well. He set her free by taking her through a truth based process. Jacob's well speaks of a spiritual place of refreshing for those like Jacob, who was a complicated and fault ridden man. God is so merciful that He provides a place for all of us who need one, such as the Samaritan woman Jesus met at the well that day.

SOCIAL INCORRECTNESS

In the culture of the first century, Jews avoided all contact with Samaritans, a group of people they despised for their history of spiritual compromises. A common Jewish phrase of derision was "You are a

Samaritan and have a demon!" John 8:48 records the Pharisees insulting Jesus with this very phrase. When Jesus requested water from the Samaritan woman at the well, He violated this social custom to engage her in a conversation that would change her life. Jesus said to her:

> **"If you knew the generosity of God and who I am, you would be asking me for a drink, and I would give you fresh, living water" (John 4:10 The Message).**

Jesus not only offered her a unique kind of water, one He called "living water," but also described the difference between it and the kind in Jacob's well:

> **"Whoever drinks of this water will thirst again,**
>
> **but whoever drinks of the water that I shall give him will never thirst. But the water that I shall give him will become in him a fountain of water springing up into everlasting life" (John 4:13-14).**

We have to marvel at the wisdom of Jesus as He spoke a word of knowledge to the Samaritan woman....

Jesus' comment touched her deep spiritual thirst. Immediately she said:

> **"Sir, give me this water, that I may not thirst, nor come here to draw" (John 4:15).**

Jesus responded:

> **"Go, call your husband, and come here."**
>
> **The woman answered and said, "I have no husband. Jesus said to her, "You have well said, 'I have no husband,'**
>
> **for you have had five husbands, and the one whom you now have is not your husband; in that you spoke truly" (John 4:16-18).**

We have to marvel at the wisdom of Jesus as He spoke a word of knowledge to the Samaritan woman about her disastrous domestic life. When He asked her to get her husband, she claimed she did not have one. He knew by the Spirit that she was in her sixth bad relationship. When she was being less than honest with Him about her circumstance, Jesus did not reproach her but affirmed the truthful part of her response, **"in that you spoke truly."** He had determined to help her see the truth of her situation because He knew that her access to the living water was directly related to her being truthful about her sin.

Jesus' method was effective. The Bible records that she received great personal benefit from her encounter with Jesus and her entire town was touched by the power of God.

The woman then left her waterpot, went her way into the city, and said to the men,

"Come, see a Man who told me all things that I ever did. Could this be the Christ?"

Then they went out of the city and came to Him (John 4:28-30).

The Spirit of truth helped the woman quench her deep spiritual thirst so completely that she left her waterpot at the well and returned home to tell people about Him. A thirsty person does not leave a waterpot at the well and return home empty-handed. She testified, **"Come, see a Man who told me all things *that I ever did*."** After meeting Jesus, she took responsibility for her own life, not blaming anyone else for her situation. He gave her living water in a way she never imagined. Her testimony had such power that those who heard her tell the story went to find Jesus, too.

Many people need and want God's transforming grace, but lack a love for the truth....

And many of the Samaritans of that city believed in Him because of the word of the woman who testified, "He told me all that I ever did" (John 4:39).

OWNING TO DISOWN: THE RELATIONSHIP OF GRACE TO TRUTH

When the Spirit of Truth delivered the woman at Jacob's well, He did so based upon an important spiritual principle that Jesus was sent to reveal:

For the law was given through Moses, but grace and truth came through Jesus Christ (John 1:17).

Grace and truth work together to transform people's lives on the basis of owning to disown. Many people need and want God's transforming grace, but lack a love for the truth, especially when it makes them look bad. It is just such truth that enables the grace to flow. When we own the truth about the kind of people we are, God releases grace for us to become the kind of people He wants us to be. The Spirit of Truth has not been sent to just reveal the truth of the Bible and correct our doctrines. He has been sent to reveal the kind of truth that set the Samaritan woman free.

KEY TO PERSONAL BREAKTHROUGH

Often a breaking precedes a breakthrough. This kind of breaking occurs when we allow the truth to break up our hard hearts. Almost thirty years ago, as a single man, I struggled in my relationship with the woman I eventually married. Our courtship was a stormy one; after a series of breakups, we decided to go our separate ways. Both of us had been through other relationships that did not work out and carried a certain amount of emotional baggage as a result, yet both of us had a strong desire for marriage.

The Lord does not ask us questions to get information.

For a number of months, I battled depression over my inability to sustain that kind of meaningful relationship. It was a dark time. One day the Lord's presence invaded my car on the way back to work from lunch. I was overjoyed to sense His presence in a way I had not known for months. Suddenly, He asked me this question: "Do you want to get married?"

I was a little incredulous that He would ask me a question about something He surely knew had dominated my thinking for a long while. One thing I was about to learn though was that the Lord does not ask us questions to get information. He asks us questions because *we* need to know something.

I said to Him, "Lord, You know I want to get married."

He replied, "What kind of girl do you want to marry?"

I said, "I want to marry the kind of girl that will be right for the ministry. She should probably be able to play the piano and be a good Sunday school teacher. You know…that kind of woman."

Instantly, the presence of the Lord left the car. I returned to the same sorry, depressed state I knew before He flooded my car moments earlier. My, was I confused!

Then, just as suddenly, He came back to me by the power of His presence and said: "Come on...what kind of girl do you really want!?"

"Oh, that..." I said to myself. Then I gave Him a vivid carnal description of the kind of woman I really had in my heart.

My *religious* answer did not move Him. My honest one did. Obviously, everything in it was not pure, but it was necessary for me to be that honest with Him in order to move forward. Within a few weeks, God restored my relationship with Donna and we were married a few months later. When I broke down and told the truth, He gave me the breakthrough I needed. We have now been married for almost thirty years.

BUY THE TRUTH

One piece of wisdom we cannot live without is found in Proverbs 23:23:

> **Buy the truth, and do not sell it, also wisdom and instruction and understanding.**

Truth is often expensive, especially when it costs our reputation. No one wants to look bad, but often that is the price we pay to move forward in the things of God. Grace is free, but the truth will cost you something.

Truth is kingdom currency; it is the coin of the realm of the kingdom of God. By embracing it we may enter boldly into the kingdom, but by refusing it we shall become darker and darker and allow the god of this world more and more access to our lives. We must listen to the Spirit of Truth and love what He has to say. ■

Robin McMillan is currently the pastor of MorningStar Fellowship Church at our H.I.M. facilities near Charlotte, North Carolina. With a unique preaching style, prophetic giftings, and a desire for the release of God's power, many are impacted by Robin's ministry. Robin and his wife, Donna, live in North Carolina and have four children: John Mark, Christopher, Andy, and Katy.

The Holy Spirit
by Larry Kreider

All Scriptures are New International Version.

The story is told of a Christian man, who lived in a poor village in the interior of his nation and had the opportunity to visit a big city. Having never experienced the use of electricity before, he was fascinated when he saw electric lightbulbs for the first time. He asked his host if he could have one to take back to his home. When he got back to his village, he hung the lightbulb on a string in his hut. He was frustrated because it wouldn't work, until a missionary explained to him that it must be plugged into a power source.

To enter into the fullness of what God has planned for our lives, we have no greater need than to be plugged into the power source of the Holy Spirit. We need the mighty baptism of the Holy Spirit. It is the gateway into a new dimension of the Spirit's presence and power in our lives, and it empowers us for ministry.

At the time of our salvation, the Holy Spirit comes to live within us. He leads and motivates us to live holy lives and delivers us from the bondage of sin. Romans 8:9 says, **"You, however, are controlled not by the sinful nature but by the Spirit, if the Spirit of God lives in you. And if anyone does not have the Spirit of Christ, he does not belong to Christ."**

During Jesus' last talk with His disciples before His trial and crucifixion, He promised them they would receive the Holy Spirit (see John 14:17). Subsequently, after His resurrection, Jesus visited the disciples and breathed on them saying, **"Receive the Holy Spirit"** **(see John 20:22).**

At that moment, the disciples were born again by the Holy Spirit. Although the disciples had already confessed Jesus as Lord and were saved according to the old covenant provisions, they could not have been born again before Jesus was raised from the dead. Jesus had to come and give them His resurrection power according to the New Covenant. Now they also believed that Jesus was raised from the dead, and their salvation was completed.

When God took a hunk of clay in the Garden of Eden and breathed on it, Adam was formed and received physical life. Here, God breathed on the disciples and gave them spiritual life. When you were convicted of your sin before you received Christ, the Holy Spirit was outside of you bringing conviction. When you received Jesus, the Holy Spirit came *inside* to live within you. But there's more! The New Testament depicts *two* distinct yet complementary aspects of receiving the Holy Spirit—the experience of the disciples receiving the Holy Spirit on "Resurrection Sunday" that we just described, and the experience they later received on "Pentecost Sunday." Let's compare the two experiences.

YOU SHALL RECEIVE POWER!

After the disciples' encounter with the Holy Spirit, when Jesus breathed on them and told them to **"receive the Holy Spirit"** in John 20:22, He made it clear that their experience was still incomplete. In His final words to them before His ascension, He commanded them not to go out and preach immediately, but to go back to Jerusalem and wait there until they were baptized in the Holy Spirit and thus given the power they needed to be effective witnesses. **"Do not leave Jerusalem, but wait for the gift my Father promised, which you have heard me speak about. For John baptized with water, but in a few days you will be baptized with the Holy Spirit. But you will receive power when the Holy Spirit comes on you; and you will be my witnesses in Jerusalem, and in all Judea and Samaria, and to the ends of the earth"** (Acts 1:4-5, 8).

So the disciples prayed and waited. During the festival of Pentecost, one hundred twenty of His disciples were gathered together in one place, and it happened! *"When the day of Pentecost came, they were all together in one place.* **Suddenly a sound like the blowing of a violent wind came from heaven and filled the whole house where they were sitting. They saw what seemed to be tongues of fire that separated**

When you received Jesus, the Holy Spirit came *inside* to live within you.

and came to rest on each of them. All of them were filled with the Holy Spirit and began to speak in other tongues as the Spirit enabled them" (Acts 2:1-4, emphasis mine).

Here, the disciples experienced the mighty baptism in the Holy Spirit. Although they had received the life of the Holy Spirit only a few weeks before when Jesus breathed on them (see John 20:22), this time they received the *baptism* in the Holy Spirit. They received a new dimension of the Holy Spirit's power.

This distinction between receiving the Holy Spirit at rebirth and receiving the *baptism in the Holy Spirit* is significant. We need to recognize the difference between having the Holy Spirit living within us and being baptized in the Holy Spirit. The baptism in the Holy Spirit is the Lord's provision for releasing the power of the Holy Spirit into the believer's life.

The baptism in the Holy Spirit is the Lord's provision for releasing the power of the Holy Spirit into the believer's life.

WANT TO BE EFFECTIVE?

I often explain the power of the Holy Spirit like this. If you mow a lawn, you can do it with scissors or with a lawn mower. It is your decision. You do not have to be baptized in the Holy Spirit to be a Christian, but like using the mower, God wants us to be effective. In fact, the early disciples of Jesus made being filled with the Holy Spirit a requirement for anyone who was to be set apart for special responsibilities in the church. **"Brothers, choose seven men from among you who are known to be full of the Spirit and wisdom. We will turn this responsibility over to them"** (Acts 6:3).

The baptism in the Holy Spirit increases the effectiveness of a Christian's witness because of a strengthening relationship with the Father, Son, and Holy Spirit that comes from being filled with the Spirit. The Holy Spirit makes the personal presence of Jesus more real to us, and it results in wanting to love and obey Him more.

A survey was taken in the Philippines some time back which found that each Christian who had received the baptism of the Holy Spirit brought thirty-six people to Christ compared to the one person led to the Lord by each Christian who had not received the Holy Spirit baptism. Why? The Spirit-baptized Christians simply had the power of God in their lives to witness with greater effect.

The difference between receiving the Holy Spirit at salvation and being baptized in the Holy Spirit can be explained like this: You can be led to a pool of water and drink from it (receive the Holy Spirit at salvation), or you can jump fully into the water (be baptized with the Holy Spirit). It's the same water (Holy Spirit), but you have a completely different experience.

During the late 1800s, evangelist Dwight L. Moody was preaching and saw the same two ladies sitting in the front row night after night. Nearly every night, they came up to him after his meetings and said, "Mr. Moody, you need to be filled with the Holy Spirit." At first he resisted their remarks. However, months later, as he walked down a street in New York City, he had an experience with God and was filled with the Holy Spirit. The results were astonishing! He preached the same sermons, but instead of two or three people getting saved at his services, hundreds, and at times thousands came to know Jesus. In his lifetime, a million people were kept out of hell because of the power of God on his life. What made the difference? The mighty baptism—infilling—of the Holy Spirit. He had received power. ■

Larry Kreider currently serves as International Director of DOVE Christian Fellowship International (DCFI), a worldwide network of churches. During the past two decades, he has trained Christian leaders nationally and internationally. He has authored several books, including *Hearing God 30 Different Ways* and *The Cry for Spiritual Father and Mothers*. Visit www.dcfi.org for more information.

The Ten Commandments of Influence

by Harry R. Jackson, Jr.

All Scriptures are New International Version.

"Does God Want You to Be Rich?" was a recent *Time* magazine cover story. *Time* contrasted the teachings of "prosperity-lite" preachers with evangelical stalwarts. They deduced that there were two opposite belief systems operative among Christians. The first group focused on receiving prosperity for oneself. The second group focused on redistributing wealth to the poor and needy. *Time* seemed to suggest that these different views on wealth were mutually exclusive. Sadly, the well-written article overlooked the obvious; Christians must prosper if they are going to have the resources to minister to the poor.

This article will attempt to answer two questions:

- How do we qualify to receive a blessing of wealth?
- What do we do with the riches that God gives us?

In the Hebrew mindset, prosperity always followed lifelong obedience. Proverbs 10:22 summarizes the concept: **"The blessing of the LORD brings wealth, and he adds no trouble to it."**

Just as there is a godly way to achieve material blessings, there are methods that the Scriptures cannot condone. Many of Solomon's teachings explain how to attain wealth the right way. As I read Proverbs 22:1-3, I realized this passage contains at least "ten commandments of influence" that can answer both questions above. Heed Solomon's words, realizing that consumption for consumption's sake can be destructive.

1. RELEASE THE TWIN SISTERS OF BLESSING

A good name is more desirable than great riches; to be esteemed is better than silver or gold (Proverbs 22:1).

The twin sisters of blessing are *a good name* and *favor*. Faithfulness is essential in creating a good name. For example, if a person has paid his bills on time he will have a good credit rating. Whether we realize it or not, we are also developing "relational" credit as we interact with people in both business and recreation. If that rating is high, we will get the "benefit of the doubt." People will assume the best about us, even in questionable situations.

I have chosen favor as a synonym for the phrase "to be esteemed." Esteem means that we honor someone. Esteem or favor is often essential to set up the opportunity to develop a good name. In addition to hard work, God's grace can produce tremendous favor for us. Favor is like a spotlight that allows us to be recognized by others. Favor may cause people to believe in our potential or respect our opinions. Favor can get us in the door, but faithfulness will keep us there and allow a deep relationship to develop.

> **E**steem or favor is often essential to set up the opportunity to develop a good name.

Several years ago, our church's real estate brokers recommended we investigate an 87-acre property just outside the eastern part of the city. As a multimillionaire, the owner did not need the money but was more interested in the vision of the people who purchased the property. Many church leaders had talked to the owner about purchasing the site. No one impressed the man until he met us. By the time our church purchased the property, the owner had given our ministry more than $300,000 in cash, equipment, and furnishings. Through the years, we have had an opportunity to share the gospel with this gentleman.

2. PURSUE OPERATIONAL WISDOM

> Rich and poor have this in common: The LORD is the Maker of them all.
>
> A prudent man sees danger and takes refuge, but the simple keep going and suffer for it (Proverbs 22:2–3).

If Donald Trump was put out on the street today without any cash, would he know how to start over and get money? He sure would!

This is because he has operational wisdom to make money. More specifically, Trump has made a fortune in real estate. His greatest skill is still in this area.

We need to develop skill and work at our craft in order to recognize and use operational wisdom. If we do not prepare, God cannot give us anything because we will not know what to do with it.

3. REFINE GODLY CHARACTER

Humility and the fear of the LORD bring wealth and honor and life.

In the paths of the wicked lie thorns and snares, but he who guards his soul stays far from them (Proverbs 22:4–5).

The secular world would call humility and the fear of the Lord as weaknesses. God, however, sees these as His bridle and saddle in our lives. Just like a well-trained horse, we cannot be useful to God's purposes until we can be easily guided by Him. Until a horse is broken of his independence, he cannot be used by his master. The inward work of progressive humility unties God's hands concerning finances and influence.

Several years ago, I read Dr. Judson Cornwall's book entitled *Pride*, which described the problems that pride brings to us. As cancer is to our natural bodies, so is pride to our spiritual systems. The more God uses us, the more we will be tempted to think that our accomplishments are due to some inherent quality in ourselves. When I hear a question like "How did Jackson pull that off?" I know that the Lord uses the foolish things to confound the wise!

This is not to discredit any of us. It is simply to acknowledge that God promotes His agenda, not our charisma or natural skills.

4. TRAIN A CHILD

Train a child in the way he should go, and when he is old he will not turn from it.

The rich rule over the poor, and the borrower is servant to the lender.

He who sows wickedness reaps trouble, and the rod of his fury will be destroyed.

A generous man will himself be blessed, for he shares his food with the poor (Proverbs 22:6–9).

These verses tell parents to train their children so that they will live out good principles all their lives. They offer three simple points that every young person should understand about the influence that comes with wealth:

1. The rich control; the poor are servants.

2. Wickedness will destroy the perpetrator in the long term.

3. Generosity to the poor releases the blessings of God.

The point is not to grow up and get rich. The point is that finances used properly enrich one's service to God.

5. SET THE RIGHT RELATIONAL ATMOSPHERE

Drive out the mocker, and out goes strife; quarrels and insults are ended.

He who loves a pure heart and whose speech is gracious will have the king for his friend (Proverbs 22:10–11).

All of us have been in workplaces that seem to breed cynicism and negativity. The Bible calls people who have been negative for a long time "*scorners*." This word in Hebrew implies arrogance and rebellion. These are people who carry a sense of controversy with them everywhere they go. They are *prima donnas* or *drama queens*. They don't have peace with God or man.

These verses tell parents to train their children so that they will live out good principles all their lives.

Sometimes we must remove these individuals from key roles in our lives. The atmosphere will change dramatically when we do. In business or ministry, it may mean a demotion. In other cases, we may need to stop receiving counsel from them. Once scorners are removed, harmony and prosperity will rest as part of the Psalm 133 blessing:

How good and pleasant it is when brothers live together in unity!

It is like precious oil poured on the head, running down on the beard, running down on Aaron's beard, down upon the collar of his robes.

It is as if the dew of Hermon were falling on Mount Zion. For there the LORD bestows his blessing, even life forevermore (Verses 1-3).

Psalm 133 people are diametrically opposed to the scorners. Scorners release controversy wherever they go. Psalm 133 people, conversely, release blessings and grace wherever they go.

If we nurture a good attitude and remain open we will attract high-level people. Over the years, I have enjoyed strong relationships with well-known leaders around the nation and the world. I have discovered that if I continue to grow and work on myself the Lord will give me such relationships. I will be called upon to support, serve, and love these leaders just because my heart is right. I consider these kinds of relationships a great blessing from God. These relationships don't just give me bragging rights, they give me serving rights.

6. KEEP YOUR SPIRITUAL EARS OPEN

Pay attention and listen to the sayings of the wise; apply your heart to what I teach (Proverbs 22:17).

This "commandment" is so clear and simple, it needs no further clarification. Keep listening to the Word of God and wise counselors.

7. TAKE CARE OF THE NEEDY

Do not exploit the poor because they are poor and do not crush the needy in court,

for the LORD will take up their case and will plunder those who plunder them (Proverbs 22:22–23).

This is an admonition for those who want to prosper: Never abuse power over the needy. Powerful people may win in an earthly court by hiring the best lawyers and outspending their opponents, but this Scripture is saying that God will ultimately even the score.

8. USE DEBT STRATEGICALLY

Do not be a man who strikes hands in pledge or puts up security for debts;

if you lack the means to pay, your very bed will be snatched from under you (Proverbs 22:26–27).

This Scripture warns against cosigning for other people's debts. If you lack the means to pay the bill, you are acting foolhardy. I do believe that there is an appropriate use of debt. Many companies must use debt to create the economy of scale to start a business. One wise business leader once told me, "If your ideas are not good enough for banks and investors to put money into your project, maybe you should not invest in it either."

9. MAINTAIN INTEGRITY EVEN WHEN IT HURTS

Do not move an ancient boundary stone set up by your forefathers (Proverbs 22:28).

Moving boundary lines is a form of stealing. Six times the Bible mentions the sin of moving boundary stones. This could be a temptation for a farmer who could easily increase the size of his farm by simply moving the stones at the boundary lines. As stated above, the long-term blessings of God follow those who do not cheat.

10. BE DILIGENT IN YOUR FIELD

Do you see a man skilled in his work? He will serve before kings; he will not serve before obscure men (Proverbs 22:29).

Young people want to leave their footprints in the sand in some way. The tenth "commandment" gives a great guiding principle. The business spoken of here is probably a God-given vocation. The man or woman who finds God's specific assignment will ultimately not live in obscurity. All of us know people who are great carpenters or doctors or teachers who have embraced the call to diligence in their fields. Not only do they seem to have been created for these jobs, they carry out their service with what looks like effortless dignity. Watching them should cause all of us to give thanks to God that He truly gives individuals specific assignments in the earth.

THE RIGHT PERSPECTIVE

It is important for believers to embrace heaven's perspective of life. We are called to take strategic posts for God in the earth. David articulated it this way: **"The earth is the LORD's, and everything in it, the world, and all who live in it" (Psalm 24:1).**

One of the ways we maintain God's witness in the earth is by allowing ourselves to be positioned by God on His chessboard. Think about it this way. None of us chooses our race, our sex, or our nation of origin. These starting points give us a godly frame of reference. Some of us have been born into less than desirable situations in order to give us a passion for social reform or ministry to people who share our origins. Others of us have been given fabulous starting points in order to make an unusual contribution to our generation.

God needs the kings and the pawns on His chessboard. No one is insignificant. A chauffeur may influence the chairman of one of America's most powerful companies.

Let's allow Him to direct our steps today. ■

Harry R. Jackson, Jr. pastors Hope Christian Church, a 3,000-member congregation in the nation's capitol with his wife, Michele. Having earned an MBA from Harvard, Jackson ministers nationally and internationally. His writing is featured in periodicals such as *Charisma, Christian Parenting, Kairos, New Man,* and the *Elijah List.* Rev. Jackson has three books to date, *In-laws, Outlaws and the Functional Family, The Warrior's Heart,* and *High Impact African-American Churches.* He has appeared on the CBS Nightly News, BET, the O'Reilly Factor on Fox, CBN, and TBN. His articles have been featured in the *Washington Times* and the *New York Sun.*

Discernment vs. Knowledge
by Nicole Roberts

In the church today, we are faced by a growing need to operate effectively in the gift of discernment. First, we must discern the times so that we can make wise decisions in our daily lives. Discernment is spiritual, not just making judgments based on information we acquire. To have discernment, we need to see by the Spirit and not by our natural eyes. The Lord has given us the gift of discernment so that we can be effective in His kingdom, but our level of effectiveness will be determined by our responses to what we discern.

For example, Jesus discerned the adulterous past of the woman at the well, and the end result was the salvation of an entire city. Many in the church today could have discerned the issues in this woman's life, but I wonder if we would have used that discernment the way the Lord did and seen the same results. Why are we not experiencing the same kind of fruit that was manifest in the life of Jesus?

WHAT IS THE ANSWER?

Romans 11:29 tells us that the gifts of God are without repentance, so we know the reason is not that we no longer have the ability to discern. In fact, it is quite the opposite. Joel 2:28 and Acts 2:17 tell us that God is going to pour out His Spirit on all flesh in the last days, and the result of this will be prophetic revelation—dreams, visions, and prophecy. This means that we should be seeing more of the gifts and fruit of the Spirit in our time than any other generation before us. We still have the gifts, and in many cases we see accurately, but we do not always respond appropriately to what the Lord is showing us. Why is this? What can we do to change the way we deal with situations so that our lives and ministries better parallel the life and ministry of Jesus?

One of the primary differences between many of our ministries today and the ministry of Jesus is that our perspectives are often based on the temporary, and the perspective of Jesus was based on the eternal. When we discern what is going on in a situation, many of us respond from a limited or even self-centered perspective, but Jesus always responded from a perspective of love, and all that He did was motivated by love. In the same situation, we might have been content to just expose the problem, but Jesus acted on what He discerned to bring a redemptive solution that ultimately led to many others believing in Him.

John Chapter 8 tells the story of a woman who was caught in the very act of adultery. It was easy enough to discern this problem because she was caught. The Pharisees brought her into the synagogue where Jesus was teaching to accuse her before Him. Imagine that, she was caught in the *very act* by the Pharisees! Jesus was teaching a large number of people in the synagogue, and they brought her into the middle of the crowd, exposed her sin, and reminded Him that, according to the Law, she should be stoned to death. Jesus chose to forgive her and not to condemn her, but the Pharisees were prepared to stone her!

They could all see the same things, but Jesus took what He saw and responded out of love....

This is a great illustration of what can so easily happen to us. In many cases, we allow the enemy to use what is being brought into the light to bring people before the Lord in accusation. Often, we will expose things and make judgments based on what we have seen. When we do this, we are taking something that the Lord has brought into the light to set someone free and using it, in a sense, to cast a stone at the person. Jesus was aware of all the things the Pharisees had seen. He knew about all the sins she had committed, and He knew about all of the issues she had in her life. They could all see the same things, but Jesus took what He saw and responded out of love, and the Pharisees responded out of condemnation and judgment.

THE HEART OF A PHARISEE

Because of their legalism, the Pharisees were not able to truly understand God's heart of mercy for this woman. They trusted in their natural knowledge and the things they thought they knew about God, but this kept them from actually seeing God as He stood in their very midst. Separated from the love and mercy of the Lord, this is what our natural knowledge will do to us as well. God has a purpose for where we are placed right now in life, and there is power released when we access God's heart for another person. It is for this reason that we should ask the Lord to show us His heart in every situation that we encounter so that we do not react out of our own knowledge because "love edifies, but knowledge puffs up" (see I Corinthians 8:1). God has designed us in such a way that we must have His love combined with our knowledge and understanding to be able to see things the way they truly are (see Philippians 1:9-10).

In addition to legalism, there are many other veils that can distort our spiritual vision, such as pride, presumption, personal opinions, old wounds, and bitterness. Interpreting through one or more of these veils will limit us to the plane of natural knowledge, which will keep us from truly understanding God's heart for the people we are around, even our most intimate relationships. II Corinthians 5:16-17 says:

> **We should ask the Lord to show us His heart in every situation that we encounter so that we do not react out of our own knowledge....**

> **Therefore, from now on, we regard no one according to the flesh. Even though we have known Christ according to the flesh, yet now we know Him thus no longer.**

> **Therefore, if anyone is in Christ, he is a new creation; old things have passed away; behold, all things have become new (NKJV).**

In this Scripture, Paul was reminding the Corinthian church that they no longer knew Jesus by the flesh, and the Lord did not intend for them to know each other by the flesh, but by the Spirit. Our lives are now hidden with Christ in God (see Colossians 3:3), so we can no longer know each other from a human perspective either. Sometimes our discernment will allow us to see the old man, but love will enable us to relate to the new man. We cannot allow ourselves to focus on where someone has been, but upon where the Lord has brought them and where He wants to take them.

SEEING THINGS A DIFFERENT WAY

Sometimes seeing through our natural eyes can cause us to miss the Lord. I was recently at a home group meeting, and a teenage girl shared a dream that she had the previous evening. In the dream, an ordinary looking man walked into the home group. She noticed him immediately and asked if he wanted to go for a walk. As they were walking, she realized that he was the Lord. She asked Him if He had a piece of paper so she could write down what He looked like so she would never forget, and she knew that no one would believe her when she told them what had happened. At the end of the dream, she gave the Lord a kiss and walked back into the house. As she suspected, when she began to tell the others what had happened, they did not believe her. She asked them why they would believe other well-known people who had come to speak there, but why they would not believe her. After this, she ran back outside and asked the Lord if she could give Him another kiss. He gladly accepted her offer and when she had kissed Him again, she went back into the meeting and the dream ended.

> **This dream illustrates the importance of being able to recognize the Lord, regardless of what He looks like to our natural minds.**

I believe this dream illustrates the importance of being able to recognize the Lord, regardless of what He looks like to our natural minds. In this dream, the Lord looked like an ordinary man, and because of that, most of the people did not recognize Him. If they had judged by the Spirit instead of by the natural, they would have known that this man was the Lord. How often does this happen to us? How often do we fail to recognize the Lord, or His heart for a situation, because we automatically judge by our natural understandings and opinions?

What would our response have been to the woman who had been caught in the act of adultery? Would we have recognized His heart for her? If we would have been in the crowd that day, would we have been among those who picked up a stone? To the natural mind, all that was evident was sin in the life of someone whom we might have deemed as being less worthy than ourselves. That was the response most everyone had. The temporary perspective said to stone her, but the eternal perspective of Jesus led Him to respond differently.

In the middle of their accusation against this woman, Jesus stooped down and began to write in the ground with His finger. He addressed the crowd and said that any man without sin could cast the first stone. Although no one knows exactly what Jesus wrote in the sand, it had enough power to send conviction through the hearts of everyone present. Jesus then asked a very powerful question: "Woman, where are your accusers? Has no man condemned you?" She answered, "No one, Lord!" And Jesus said, "I do not condemn you either. Go on your way and from now on sin no more" (see John 8:10-11). This statement is extremely powerful. If we do not bring accusation against each other, then He does not bring accusation either. If we do not condemn each other, then there is no condemnation because He does not condemn us either.

We have the ability to release either judgment or mercy in people's lives.

This is the kind of power that we carry. We have the ability to release either judgment or mercy in people's lives. Whatever Jesus wrote in the sand was enough to show the Pharisees that they too needed mercy. He wanted them to stop accusing her, because if they did, He would *not* have to judge her. In verse 15, Jesus said to them: "You set yourselves up to judge according to the flesh by what you see. You condemn by external, human standards. *I do not set myself up to judge or condemn or sentence anyone.*" Hebrews 7:25 tells us that Jesus is interceding on our behalf before the Father, not accusing us. We are the only ones who have the power to bring accusation before the throne of God.

THE HEART OF GOD

The blueprints of God's heart for how we should respond to what we discern are clearly seen in this story. There she was standing in the middle of the synagogue, probably without any of her clothes, and her sin and shame were blatantly obvious. Jesus could see all of this, but He looked past the natural. He saw the results of her sin and the impact it was having in her life, but He did not focus on the sin itself. Because of this, His response to her was: "I do not condemn you."

James 3:17 tells us that:

> **But the wisdom that comes from heaven is first of all pure; then peace-loving, considerate, submissive, full of mercy and good fruit, impartial and sincere (NIV).**

This wisdom from heaven is what we are called to have as we minister the love of Jesus to the world. As we grow in our understanding of this kind of wisdom, we will begin to see that our gift of discernment is actually a tool that God has given us to enable us to show His love. When we discern things about another person or situation, the Lord has revealed this to us so we can respond with His love and help bring a solution. We can take what He has given us to accurately see into a situation or a person's heart, and make a lasting change. ∎

Nicole Roberts is from Orange County, California and is a recent graduate of the MorningStar School of Ministry. She has a heart for the prophetic ministry, evangelism, prophetic counseling, and deliverance. Nicole currently lives in Moravian Falls, North Carolina with her husband, Mike. She is on staff at MorningStar's Wilkesboro church.

The Baptism of the Holy Spirit in Missions

by Che Ahn

All Scriptures are New International Version.

The late John Wimber, founder of the Vineyard movement of churches, coined a wonderful term some twenty years ago: *power evangelism*. He wrote a book by that name, which I regret to say is currently out of print. He was a pioneer in helping the last generation to understand how the gifts we have in the Holy Spirit are the most powerful tools we can employ in sharing the gospel. His message, however, was not new—just perhaps forgotten.

We know that Jesus Himself received the Holy Spirit, coming upon Him as a dove at His baptism in the Jordan (see Luke 3:21–23). The Spirit then led Jesus into the wilderness to be tempted, and He overcame all temptation. Jesus then returned from the wilderness in great power of the Spirit (see Luke 4:14) and began His ministry in the miraculous.

Even though Jesus' disciples were with Him throughout His entire earthly ministry, they, too, needed something more. He commanded His disciples to receive the power of the Holy Spirit by waiting in the upper room (see Acts 1:8). With this gift, **"the apostles performed many miraculous signs and wonders among the people. . . [And] more and more men and women believed in the Lord and were added to their number"** (Acts 5:12, 14). The Apostle Paul declared, **"My message and my preaching were not with wise and persuasive words, but with a demonstration of the Spirit's power"** (I Corinthians 2:4).

The Holy Spirit has always been God's intended means of bringing a visible demonstration of His kingdom to this earth. The gospel was never meant to be dependent upon the words of man alone—no matter how eloquent or well-intentioned.

Yet many people still believe that such powerful work of the Holy Spirit as I have just described has ceased. Most notably, cessationists believe that the miracle-working power and distinct infilling of the Holy Spirit were necessary to establish the fledgling church. Now that the church is established and the canon of Scripture is closed, cessationists believe that such power manifestations or infilling are no longer necessary or available, that they have ceased.

By way of explanation, I would like to offer some inspiring experiences of well-known, modern era Christians who received a *distinct* filling of the Holy Spirit. Their evangelistic influence for Christ increased exponentially afterward. This experience is captured by many different terms and phrases, including *being baptized in the Holy Spirit, receiving the gift of the Holy Spirit, and being filled with the Holy Spirit.* Regardless of the terminology, the bottom line is that each of these believers received the *power* of the Holy Spirit.

I emphasize the word *distinct* because the experience of receiving the Holy Spirit most often happens at a completely different time following someone's conversion experience. I personally believe God's optimum plan is for this to happen at the *same time* one is saved (see Acts 2:38), but the overwhelming majority of the testimonies I have read or heard, including the stories which follow, seem to indicate otherwise.

The bottom line is that each of these believers received the *power* of the Holy Spirit.

Let's begin with D.L. Moody. I have read many accounts of how this famous nineteenth-century evangelist received the power of the Holy Spirit, but this description by the late author Catherine Marshall is my favorite.

The year 1871 saw Dwight L. Moody apparently a great success as an evangelist. His tabernacle drew the largest congregations in Chicago. But according to Moody's own estimate of those years, he was "a great hustler" and this work was being done "largely in the energy of the flesh." Two humble Free Methodist women, Auntie Cook and Mrs. Snow, used to attend these meetings and sit on the front row. Moody could not help seeing that they were praying during most of his services. Finally he spoke to the women about it. "Yes," they admitted, "we have been praying for you." "Why me? Why not for the unsaved?" the evangelist retorted, a bit nettled. "Because you need the power of the Spirit," was their answer. After some weeks of this, Mr. Moody invited the women to his office to talk about it. "You spoke of power for service," he prodded them. "I thought I had it. I wish you would tell me what you mean."

So Mrs. Snow and Auntie Cook told Moody what they knew about the baptism of the Holy Spirit. Then the three Christians prayed together— and the women left. From that hour "there came a great hunger in my soul," Moody was to say later. "I really felt that I did not want to live if I could not have this power for service." One late autumn day in 1871 Dwight L. Moody was in New York (on his way to England) walking up Wall Street. Suddenly, in the midst of the bustling crowds, his prayer was answered: The power of God fell on him so overwhelmingly that he knew he must get off the street. Spotting a house he recognized, Moody knocked on the door and asked if he might have a room by himself for a few hours. Alone there, such joy came upon him that "at last he had to ask God to withhold His hand, lest he die on the spot from very joy." From that hour, Moody's ministry was never the same. He went on to England for what was to be the first of many evangelistic campaigns there. People thronged to North London to hear him. "The sermons were no different," Moody summarized. "I did not present any new truths, and yet hundreds were converted. I would not now be placed back where I was before that blessed experience if you should give me all the world." The evangelist was to live another twenty-eight years, and "to reduce the population of hell by a million souls." Through the Moody Bible Institute, the Moody Press, the Northfield Conferences, the Northfield and Mt. Hermon Schools, the vigor and power of his work continues to this day (Marshall).

> **The power of God fell on him so overwhelmingly that he knew he must get off the street.**

Charles Finney, one of the greatest evangelists of all time, shares in his autobiography how the Holy Spirit came upon him after he returned from revisiting the woods where he was converted:

I returned to the front office, and found that the fire that I had made of large wood was nearly burned out. But as I turned and was about to take a seat by the fire, I received a mighty baptism of the Holy Ghost. Without any expectation of it, without ever having the thought in my mind that there was any such thing for me, without any recollection that I had ever heard the thing mentioned by any person in the world, the Holy Spirit descended upon me in a manner that seemed to go through me, body and soul. I could feel the impression, like a wave of electricity, going through and through me. Indeed it seemed to come in waves and waves of liquid love; for I could not express it in any other way. It seemed like the very breath of God. I can recollect distinctly that it seemed to fan me, like immense wings. No words can express the wonderful love that was shed abroad in my heart. I wept aloud with joy and love; and I do not know but I should say, I literally bellowed out the unutterable gushings of my heart. These waves came over me, and over me, and over me, one after the other, until I recollect I cried out, "I shall die if these waves continue to pass over me." I said, "Lord, I cannot bear any more;" yet I had no fear of death (Finney 1876, 20–21).

Aimee Semple McPherson was a remarkable healing evangelist in the early twentieth century and the founder of the Four Square denomination. This account was written by Mike Epstein:

> **No words can express the wonderful love that was shed abroad in my heart.**

Aimee . . . took up her vigil kneeling by the Morris chair . . . It was there she heard God's voice: "Now child, cease your striving and begging; just begin to praise Me, and in simple childlike faith, receive ye the Holy Ghost." Aimee did what she was told. She whispered, "Glory, glory," and each time the word seemed to come from a graver source within her and in a deeper voice. At last the words of praise came thundering out of her, resonating from her feet to her diaphragm and out the top of her head. Her hands and arms began to twitch and tremble, gently at first and then more violently, and then her whole body was shaking with the power of the Holy Spirit. She recalls that this seemed altogether natural; she had seen how the storage batteries she experimented with in school hummed and shook and trembled under the power of electricity. Her image is precise, and weirdly modern . . . She trembled, and she quaked, until at last she slipped to the floor and "was lying under the power of God, but felt as though caught up and floating upon the billowing clouds of glory. . . ." Then her tongue began to move in her mouth . . . vowels came howling and then a distinct syllable, and another, stammering, until they flowed in a sentence Aimee could not understand. "Then suddenly, out of my innermost being flowed rivers of praise in other tongues as the Spirit gave utterance" (see Acts 2:4) (Epstein 1993, pg. 53).

My final favorite is that of Billy Graham (my hero!). In William Martin's outstanding biography of Dr. Graham, he gives this account of Billy's experience in being filled with the Holy Spirit:

> *Billy was visiting a Welsh evangelist, Stephen Olford, and Olford shared with Billy his experience with the Holy Spirit . . . those marvelous eyes glistening with tears, and he (Billy) said, "Stephen, I see it. That's what I want. That is what I need in my life." Olford suggested they "pray this through," and both men fell on their knees. I can hear Billy pouring out his heart in a prayer of total dedication to the Lord. Finally, he said, "My heart is so flooded with the Holy Spirit," and we went from praying to praising. We were laughing and praising God, and he was walking back and forth across the room, crying out, "I have it. I'm filled. This is the turning point in my life." And he was a new man (Martin 1991, 98–99).*

The year was 1947, a year before Billy would be catapulted into international fame as the greatest evangelist of modern time. Perhaps this is the hour for your experience. If you have never known the fullness of the Holy Spirit's power or the kind of hunger described by these generals of the faith, ask the Lord to baptize you now with the fire of His Holy Spirit. It is not for some, but for all, and it is the very down payment and first fruit of the supernatural life that is for you to live today and for eternity (see Ephesians 1:13-14). ∎

This is an excerpt from Che Ahn's book Fire Evangelism, published by Chosen, a division of Baker Publishing Group, 2006.

Che Ahn and his wife, Sue, are the senior pastors of Harvest Rock Church in Pasadena, California. Che is also the founder and president of Harvest International Ministries, a worldwide apostolic network of over fifteen hundred churches in over thirty nations. Che is the author of numerous books including *Into the Fire, How to Pray for Healing,* and *Fire Evangelism.* Che and his wife, Sue, have four children.

Reigning With Christ
by Angie Weaver

All Scriptures are New King James Version.

Therefore my people have gone into captivity, because they have no knowledge; their honorable men are famished, and their multitude dried up with thirst (Isaiah 5:13).

Many in the church today are being held captive spiritually, not because of the enemy's power, but because we do not clearly understand our authority and calling in Christ. This was also true during the Apostle Peter's time, and he encouraged us that one of our most important goals as Christians should be to make our call and election sure (see II Peter 1:10). As we begin to understand the hope of His calling, we will begin to walk in an abundant life of freedom and power.

GOD'S CALL

In I Corinthians 6:2-3, the Apostle Paul said that Christians would one day judge the world as well as heavenly beings. He was not just referring to leaders or mature Christians, but he was talking about the entire church body. In context, Paul was rebuking the Corinthian church for not understanding their ability to discern justice among themselves when they were destined to one day judge the whole earth! They were wasting valuable opportunities to grow in wisdom for the age to come. In Ephesians 3:10 he said:

...that now the manifold wisdom of God might be made known by the church to the principalities and powers in the heavenly places.

Heavenly beings actually learn the wisdom and counsel of God through us, the church. Despite how little many of us feel we know about God and His justice, we are all still called to rule with Him. Angels are living beings who see God, dwell in His manifest presence, and witness His justice and righteousness firsthand. Compared to us, angels have long since perceived the Lord better than we have and they have a better understanding of His ways. However, God chose to adopt us as His sons and daughters, called us to be intimately acquainted with Him, and placed His very Spirit *within* us. We have become God's heirs with Christ and are called to rule the earth with Him (see Revelation 1:6).

Asaph, the author of Psalm 82, had a deep conviction that God has called us to rule and reign with Him:

> **God stands in the congregation of the mighty; He judges among the gods.**
>
> **How long will you judge unjustly, and show partiality to the wicked?**
>
> **Defend the poor and fatherless; do justice to the afflicted and needy.**
>
> **Deliver the poor and needy; free them from the hand of the wicked.**
>
> **They do not know, nor do they understand; they walk about in darkness; all the foundations of the earth are unstable.**
>
> **I said, "You are gods, and all of you are children of the Most High.**
>
> **"But you shall die like men, and fall like one of the princes" (Psalm 82:1-7).**

We have become God's heirs with Christ and are called to rule the earth with Him....

In this Psalm, the author describes God's assessment of the state of His people, whom he describes as "gods." He wonders how long the congregation will withhold His justice on the earth. Asaph perceives that the assembly is oblivious to their authority to exercise God's rule in the earth and that the very foundations of the earth are unstable because of it. In intercession, Asaph turns to the assembly and prophesies, declaring their inheritance as God's sons and daughters. He leaves them with a warning that if they continue being ignorant of their authority in the earth, they would "die like men and fall like princes." In other words, they would die having no significant eternal inheritance. They would be like people who never achieved their goal, princes who never achieved kingship. Asaph ends his Psalm by taking God's call personally; he began walking in the authority that was available to him and declared God's rule over the earth.

OUR CHOICE

We know that, generally speaking, royalty comes by birth and not by our achievements. It does not matter how badly we mess up in our lives—God has still called us to rule with His Son if our faith is in Him.

God has still called us to rule with His Son if our faith is in Him.

So the question is not whether we are called, but whether we will choose to take up the call. Our choice determines the extent to which we activate our inheritance and authority. God does not force Himself on us, but allows us to choose Him of our own free will. The day of God's power is not marked by force, but when His people volunteer or choose to participate with Him. Psalm 110:3 says:

> **Your people shall be volunteers in the day of Your power.**

We now walk in authority by faith, but when Christ returns, our authority and position will be evident to all. It is easy to become passive and lax in our present lives, because there seems to be no real accountability or certainty of our authority. That is, unless we *choose* to be accountable and to live with conviction. We see this in the story of Esau and Jacob. Esau presumed he did not need to maintain his place of blessing because the tradition was for the birthright to go to the firstborn. However, Jacob received the promises because, despite the tradition, he chose to aggressively pursue them. Jesus said it is the violent who take the kingdom by force (see Matthew 11:12).

The Israelites were, in essence, a nation of "kings." When settling in their land, they had no king ruling over them. Instead, they were taught God's law by the priests, training them to be responsible for themselves and each other. They eventually saw their need for a king. This was not out of a conviction of wanting someone to lead them in righteousness, but rather in desiring someone who could do the job for them so they could get on with their lives. Learning about God by studying the Law became tiresome and they no longer cared for each other. They assumed they would never lose their inheritance because they had God's Word. But by choosing to not participate with God's Word, they forfeited their inheritance by a slow process of defeat. When Jesus came, He reemphasized the Word that establishes kingship in each one, which is to love God with all our being and love our neighbor as ourselves (see Deuteronomy 6:5; Leviticus 19:18; Matthew 22:37-39).

THE TRAINING

We grow into our inheritance through prayer and intimacy with God. This requires humility and faith, like that of a child. Children spend hours of every day using their imaginations. Without realizing it, they are developing problem-solving skills by creating real-life scenarios in their playtime. As adults, we see this as childish and beneath us because their imagined scenarios are our reality. That is why many of us have such a hard time waiting on God in prayer. Either we are too overwhelmed with our circumstances, or we feel like we are sufficient in and of ourselves.

> **We grow into our inheritance through prayer and intimacy with God.**

Prayer stretches us because we have to deny what looks like reality and believe in what is not seen. We have to use our imaginations and believe that God can create something that does not yet exist in the situations of our lives. We have to become like children if we want to recognize and pursue our kingdom inheritance. Jesus says in Matthew 18:3-4:

"Assuredly I say to you, unless you are converted and become as little children, you will by no means enter the kingdom of heaven.

"Therefore whoever humbles himself as this little child is the greatest in the kingdom of heaven."

Just as children develop problem-solving skills by using their imaginations, prayer allows us to discover God and the justice and mercy behind all of His actions. One example of this is found in the life of Abraham. Abraham was given a promise that he would be the father of a nation that would bless the whole earth, and that "kings" would descend from him (see Genesis 12:2-3, 17:6). He was being called into Christ's inheritance of kingship before this was fully established on the earth.

Abraham experienced God's love firsthand and it left an everlasting impression on him to rule with mercy....

By blessing Abraham, the Lord was not only inviting him into the fellowship of His presence, He was also inviting him to come and take counsel with Him concerning the people of the earth. In Genesis 18, the Lord discussed with Abraham the coming judgment on Sodom and Gomorrah. Through intercession, Abraham received hands-on training in "judging nations."

Most of us may have wanted God to destroy Sodom and Gomorrah because of the kinds of sins that were being committed. Most of us would probably have wondered why Christians would be settling in such a "God-forsaken" land. However, God's dealings with Abraham through this situation dispelled all myths concerning His being a tyrant or desiring to see people suffer for their sins. Abraham experienced God's love firsthand and it left an everlasting impression on him to rule with mercy, just as he witnessed in God.

See then that you walk circumspectly, not as fools but as wise,

redeeming the time (making the most of every oppor-tunity, NIV), because the days are evil.

Therefore do not be unwise but understand what the will of the Lord is.

And do not be drunk with wine, in which is dissipation; but be filled with the Spirit (Ephesians 5:15-18).

Another essential aspect of our training is learning to live life in the Spirit. In this passage of Scripture, Paul is exhorting the church to be filled with the Spirit so we can understand God's will, enabling us to make the most of every opportunity or redeem time. By understanding God's ways, Abraham began redeeming time, creating an opportunity for Lot and his family to escape judgment. As we spend time in God's presence, walk in the Spirit, and grow in the understanding of His will, we are redeeming time! People's lives are being changed, they are being covered by mercy, and they are experiencing heaven.

The Holy Spirit has been eagerly waiting to fill and be a part of men's hearts and minds since He first hovered over the formlessness of the earth. Being filled with the Spirit is the key to walking in the greater works or kingdom power. Jesus only lived three years filled by the Spirit after His baptism, and in that span of time did the greatest works known to mankind. Imagine what could happen if we were all filled and led by the Spirit as Christ was, for a longer period of time on the earth!

> Another essential aspect of our training is learning to live life in the Spirit.

The Spirit Himself bears witness with our spirit that we are children of God,

and if children, then heirs—heirs of God and joint heirs with Christ, if indeed we suffer with Him, that we may also be glorified together.

For the earnest expectation of creation eagerly waits for the revealing of the sons of God (Romans 8:16-17, 19).

We are powerless without the Spirit because He is the witness of our adoption by God. He is the nature of God which we were baptized into when we made the decision to follow Christ. Being filled with the Spirit is walking in the conviction that God is our Father and we are His children. This is how Jesus accessed heaven on earth. He was dedicated to the fact that He was God's Son and, therefore, had the right to walk in authority and power. Creation knows who the sons of God are because they are marked by redemption and the result of their presence is peace and stability on earth. Jesus said in Matthew 5:9:

> **"Blessed are the peacemakers, for they shall be called sons of God."**

CONCLUSION

Having been born of God, we are called to walk as kings on the earth. However, the Bible says that many are called but few are chosen (see Matthew 20:16). If we draw near to God, He will draw near to us (see James 4:8). We enter into our inheritance by choosing to accept God's call. We activate and grow in our authority on the earth through intimacy with God and living our lives filled with the Holy Spirit. By being filled and walking in the conviction of the Holy Spirit, we are bridging heaven and earth and hastening the day of Christ's return to rule and reign over the earth! ■

Angie Weaver is a graduate of the MorningStar School of Ministry and has been involved at MorningStar in the Charlotte area for the past five years. She co-leads the Prophetic Intercession Ministry and is a Jr. High and Youth leader. Her passion is to see people find their purpose and be released in their gifts and callings. She has a heart for the prophetic, intercession, and the presence of the Lord. Angie lives in Pineville, North Carolina and works as a nanny.

The OVERCOMING LIFE

Truth for a Victorious Life

Hearing Affects Speaking
by Hombre Liggett

A Spirit-filled ministry is a ministry that is led by God's Spirit. To obtain a ministry that is led by God's Spirit, we must strive to hear God's instruction continually. Jesus' ministry, which is our greatest example, was based on what Jesus knew God to be saying and doing.

> **Therefore Jesus answered and was saying to them, "Truly, truly, I say to you, the Son can do nothing of Himself, unless it is something He sees the Father doing; for whatever the Father does, these things the Son also does in like manner" (John 5:19).**

> **So Jesus said, "...I do nothing on My own initiative, but I speak these things as the Father taught Me.**

> **"And...I always do the things that are pleasing to Him" (John 8:28-29,** emphasis mine).

It should be our goal to know what God is doing and then join in with Him. When we are walking out the very words and actions of God, then our lives become a greater extension of His ministry. That is what largely defines Spirit-filled ministry. It is discerning what the Holy Spirit is saying and doing, and then speaking and doing it in obedience.

SPEECH IMPEDIMENTS

In Mark 7:32-33, a group of people brought to Jesus a man who was deaf and did not speak well. We can learn more by looking closer at these events in Scripture.

They brought to Him one who was deaf and spoke with difficulty, and they implored Him to lay His hand on him (Mark 7:32).

In the natural, when someone has hearing difficulties they will oftentimes develop a speech impediment. Hearing poorly can eventually affect the ability to speak well. This is also true spiritually.

When we are not pursuing to hear and know God's voice, we develop spiritual deafness. If a person's spiritual hearing is compromised, then they will develop a spiritual speech impediment. To speak well, we must hear well. Our ability to hear the Holy Spirit affects our ability to accurately speak for God.

> **O**ur lives are to be for the Lord and His ministry, and we should always be trying to align ourselves more with Him.

The speech impediments developed from a lack of hearing God can also manifest throughout many areas in a believer's life. People communicate with much more than their words, and there are many other things we do that can clearly articulate the Lord to others.

Not listening to God can impede our boldness, obedience, worship, and ability to honor Jesus. It can result in speaking falsely, or not giving plain, straightforward answers. Impure stories, gossip, and false testimonies can also develop from a lack of hearing the Lord.

Our lives are to be for the Lord and His ministry, and we should always be trying to align ourselves more with Him. If we are producing some of these hindrances, then a cure for these can be correcting our hearing problem.

CORRECTING OUR HEARING

Jesus took him aside from the crowd, by himself, and put His fingers into his ears, and after spitting, He touched his tongue with the saliva (Mark 7:33).

Jesus took this man away from everyone else to be with Him alone. The first step in getting a spiritual hearing problem fixed is to get away from everything and everyone, and spend some time alone with the Lord. A common reason for not hearing the Lord's voice is not seeking His face and spending time with Him. Jesus promises to anyone who seeks Him that they will find Him, and that He rewards those who seek His face.

We are always giving our time to someone or something. If we are not giving time to the Lord, then something has moved in front of Him in our lives. This happens to most people at some point. When we find that we do not have Jesus at the top of our priorities, then we need to repent from putting something before the Lord and not seeking after Him first.

We cannot say, "If God would only fix my hearing problem, then my impediments would be corrected." Like many children, we do not hear because we do not listen. Simply begin to ask God to speak to you and then listen. If you begin to get alone with God and spend time with Him, then He will get personal with your ears (just as He did with the deaf man in Mark 7).

Prayer is one of the most important aspects of a relationship with the Lord.

In Mark 7:33, the Lord stuck His fingers in this man's ears. As unorthodox as that may sound, it hints of gaining the presence of God in our ears. This is more than just acquiring the ability to hear the Lord. As our hearing becomes more attuned to His voice, then our mouths will begin to be anointed with the wetness of His words. With corrected hearing, the Lord will touch our tongues with His saliva and begin to heal speech impediments throughout our lives.

ALONE WITH GOD

There are specific ways to spend time with God. Prayer is one of the most important aspects of a relationship with the Lord. I have heard it taught that the devil will encourage Christians to attend church and Bible studies as long as they do not pray. The enemy will do whatever he can to keep us from committed and consistent prayer.

Prayer helps us to define God's voice. When believers become committed to a life of prayer, then they become an exponential threat to the enemy. When we develop our ability to know and hear God's voice and begin to do what we are hearing, then the Spirit-filled ministry of Christ will begin to flow through our lives. This causes the advancement of God's kingdom, which is automatically damaging to the devil's strongholds.

Hearing God's voice is not just something that needs to be *obtained*, but it must be *sustained*. We can do this by committing to a life of prayer and by reading, knowing, and meditating upon Scripture and establishing times of fasting in our lives.

The Lord will honor those who diligently pursue Him and know Him. He has given each of us a unique opportunity to partner with Him in Jesus' ministry by making us the body of Christ. Our own body does what the mind tells it; likewise, the body of Christ is to be influenced by its Head, Jesus Christ (see Ephesians 5:23, Colossians 1:18).

Jesus wants to fill us daily with His Spirit and give us divine opportunities to do the very things He is doing. God will privilege us to do more than just work for Him. He is calling us to do and say precisely what He is doing and saying. That is the ministry of Christ which is Spirit-filled ministry.

The Bible tells us that God is a rewarder of those who seek Him (see Hebrews 11:6). What greater reward is there than to do the very things our Father in heaven is doing? ■

Hombre Liggett is ordained through MorningStar Fellowship of Ministries and is the founding pastor of Church of the Harvest, located in Dover, Ohio. Hombre's heart is to lead the members of the body of Christ into prophetic worship, equipped to fulfill their purpose, and provide a platform for them to function. The foundation of his twelve-year ministry is the love of God and the unity of the Spirit.

Canvas
by Sarah Williams

Stretched taut, I await the Painter.
I wonder if He will ever come for me?
In a room full of paintings far
more beautiful than I,
will He ever see me?
His palette an array of beauty—
His brush fine and precise—
will I ever taste the brilliance
of color or feel the tickle of
His brushes?
Can I be repaired?
My edges are worn.
My paint is chipped and cracked.
Deformed and discarded,
I am a reject.
Shoved carelessly into a corner,
facing a dusty mirror,
forced to stare into my
disgusting reality,
dark and alone.
I cannot see the other artworks,
but I know they are perfect.
I long to be one of them.
The Painter arrives.

I hear Him bustle about the room,
moving furniture and paintings,
searching for the perfect canvas.
It will be one of them.
Silence.
He has found His piece.
Yet suddenly I feel the dust flutter
around me.
His seasoned hands gently
grasp my frame.
It cannot be.
Delicately, He places me on His
easel facing the sun.
I am blinded—
I cannot see the other paintings,
but I no longer care.
The Painter has chosen me.
His calloused fingers explore me,
crawling across me with love and
childlike wonder.
He brushes away the cobwebs.
I am His.
And as I feel the colors creep into
my pores,
I see the Painter.
Just as I am. ∎

Sarah Williams is nineteen years old and is currently a first
year student at the MorningStar School of Ministry. Sarah not
only hopes to further develop her writing, but she has a heart to
travel and help impoverished children come to know the love of
Jesus. She currently resides in North Carolina.

The Age of the Holy Spirit
by Rick Joyner

When I first became a Christian and read in the Bible about the different encounters with God that men had, I could hardly contain the desire for one myself. I suppose every Christian dreams about walking with God like Adam did in the Garden, or meeting with Him face-to-face like Moses did. Of course, if there could have been anything better than this it would have been to be one of Jesus' disciples and be close to Him when He walked the earth as a man. However, we have been given something better than such encounters—the Lord does not just visit us, but He has given us His Holy Spirit to live inside of us! This is what the Lord meant when He made the remarkable statement in John 16:7:

> **"But I tell you the truth, it is to your advantage that I go away; for if I do not go away, the Helper shall not come to you; but if I go, I will send Him to you."**

Think about this. The Lord told His disciples that having the Helper, the Holy Spirit, come to them was more to their advantage than having Him walking with them in the flesh! God does not just visit us, He lives in us. How awesome is the gift of the Holy Spirit! Every Christian should be in a continual state of marveling just as Mary, the mother of Jesus, must have been when she knew God Himself was growing in her.

THE REALITY TEST

Yet, are we walking in this truth? A good test would be to consider how different our day would have been if we had risen out of bed and Jesus had been standing there physically manifested. The truth is that Jesus was there and is even with us right now by the Holy Spirit. Do we see Him? Do we live in constant fellowship with Him? He never leaves us or forsakes us. He is as present with us right now by the Spirit as He ever was with Adam, Moses, or His own disciples when He walked the earth.

Of course, those who are still natural think of seeing as that which they can see with their physical eyes, but those who are maturing spiritually live even more by what they see with "the eyes of their heart" (see Acts 28:27), as Paul called it, or their spiritual eyes. If we are walking by the Spirit what we see with our spiritual eyes will be more real to us than what we see with our natural eyes. Again, even better than having Jesus with us in the flesh, is having the Holy Spirit living inside of us. This is a truth that will become increasingly manifest in His people.

THE GOD WHO IS WITH US

We are in the age of the Holy Spirit. Since Jesus ascended, the Holy Spirit is the God who is on the earth during this age. This does not mean that Jesus cannot or does not come to the earth. He obviously makes visitations from time to time, just as we see on at least two occasions in the life of the Apostle Paul in the Book of Acts, and as He has done for many throughout the church age. However, the work of God in this age is done almost entirely through the Holy Spirit. Therefore, to know the Holy Spirit, and be able to recognize Him and His works, is essential for being used by God in this age.

Some would protest that such a focus on the Spirit is contrary to the Spirit, who was not given to reveal Himself, but to lead us to Jesus. This is true, that the purpose of the Spirit is to lead us to Jesus. However, when Jesus or the apostles spoke of the Holy Spirit, were they not speaking by the Spirit?

In a way, this is more real than many can understand—to have the Holy Spirit is to have the Son and the Father. They are one or in perfect unity. To really understand the Holy Spirit we must begin by understanding His whole intent which is to reveal the Son, just as it was the Son's whole intent to reveal the Father. Our intent to understand the Spirit better is to be better used by Him to reveal the Son.

THE SPIRIT MOVES

In the very first mention of the Holy Spirit in Scripture, Genesis 1:2, we are told "**...the Spirit of God was moving....**" This is a revelation of the basic nature of the Holy Spirit—He moves. He is not static, but kinetic. This is why His great works are referred to as "*moves* of the Holy Spirit." Those who are filled with Him will follow Him and abide in

Him—likewise ever moving, going somewhere, and doing something. There is only one place in Scripture where the Spirit stops moving—when He descended and rested upon Jesus. Jesus is our destination. Until we are like Him, and do the works that He did, we need to keep moving, growing, and expanding.

The true Christian life is never static, but growing, expanding, ever fresh and exciting. This does not mean that we do not rest, but we find our rest by being yoked with the Lord. A yoke speaks of work and to do His work with Him is the greatest way to find true rest and true refreshment. There is nothing more exciting or invigorating than to have the Spirit of God use us.

Obviously, to be led by the Spirit, we will be going somewhere because someone who is sitting still does not need to be led. Where is He leading you? The manna from heaven is fresh every day. The true Christian life can never be stale or static.

The true Christian life is never static, but growing, expanding, ever fresh and exciting.

THE SPIRIT SPEAKS

Acts 2:17-18 gives us another important aspect of the work of the Holy Spirit as we enter the "last days":

"And it shall be in the last days," God says, "That I will pour forth of My Spirit upon all mankind; and your sons and your daughters shall prophesy, and your young men shall see visions, and your old men shall dream dreams;

even upon My bond-slaves, both men and women, I will in those days pour forth of My Spirit and they shall prophesy."

Here we see that when the Spirit is poured out in the last days it will be accompanied by dreams, visions, and prophecy. A good biblical and historical case could be made that every time the Spirit is poured out, the ways that God speaks to His people accompany the outpouring. However, even more basic is our need to understand that God is the ultimate great Communicator. A great part of the Spirit's work is to communicate to God's people what is on His heart and mind.

When I say "heart" and "mind" it is because God does not only communicate what He is doing, but also why He is doing it. His ultimate purpose is not just our obedience, but for us to be of one mind and heart with Him. The ultimate heart of God is Christ, and the ultimate mind of God is Christ. The ultimate purpose of God is for all things to be summed up in Christ, just as we are told in Ephesians 1:9-10:

> He made known to us the mystery of His will, according to His kind intention which He purposed in Him
>
> with a view to an administration suitable to the fulness of the times, that is, the summing up of all things in Christ, things in the heavens and things upon the earth. In Him....

His ultimate purpose is not just our obedience, but for us to be of one mind and heart with Him.

Therefore, it will always be the Spirit's basic intent to reveal Christ, to lead us to Him, and to work all things so that we will be conformed to His image. As we read here, the conclusion of all things will be to be summed up in Christ. Everything the Father loves, esteems, and honors is in His Son. The Spirit is the most basic manifestation of the Father's love for His Son, and the power of that love. If we are truly Spirit-filled people, this will also be our focused devotion in all we do because this is the focused devotion of the Holy Spirit.

How does this work practically, considering that we have to work and live in this world with much of our time spent concentrating on such things? We should also consider that Jesus Himself learned a trade, worked, and lived a very practical life in this world before beginning His ministry. However, without question, He did everything that He did with godly character. We, too, should consider it a part of our training to do all we do with godly character. This may all seem natural and down to earth, but is that not what Jesus did by coming to the earth? This, too, is Christlikeness, and is a prerequisite to being used in a more spiritual and supernatural ministry.

In this we see that even Jesus, the Son of God, obviously perfect in character, still had the Holy Spirit come upon Him and empower Him for His ministry. If even Jesus, the Son of God, needed the Holy Spirit, how much more do we?

There is no reputable record of Jesus performing a single miracle before the Holy Spirit descended upon Him. Until then, He lived a basic human life. He was therefore fully in touch with all of our weaknesses and limitations. However, when the Spirit came upon Him, He was no longer limited to the natural laws of this world, but lived and revealed the higher laws of the spiritual realm.

Jesus is the Door so that mankind can leap beyond the natural realm to become a part of a new creation.

Jesus is the Door so that mankind can leap beyond the natural realm to become a part of a new creation. The new creation is the bridge between the spiritual and natural realms, but our calling is to grow in the knowledge of the spiritual until we are actually more at home in the spiritual realm than the natural.

Even the natural man was created to have a hunger for the spiritual because we were created to have a relationship with God who is Spirit. That is why there is such an interest in and even a yearning for the supernatural in every human being, whether they acknowledge it or not. To follow this pursuit by being led by the Spirit of God will lead to the highest fulfillment we can ever know as human beings. This is the ultimate quest—the most noble cause.

The atonement of the cross was required because of the Fall, but God seekers and theologians have often speculated about whether Jesus would have come to the earth to live as a man and become the Door for the new creation even if the atonement had not been necessary. It does seem that the Lord always intended for mankind to be the bridge between the natural and spiritual creations, but for a Way to be made for mankind to actually take on the divine nature, and become sons and daughters of God, is still an incomprehensible marvel even to the angels.

Obviously, the Lord Jesus could have bound Satan and taken His authority over the earth immediately after His resurrection. He had, as the "last Adam," purchased mankind, the earth, and all it contained with His sacrifice. The atonement was complete and fully accomplished. He has waited this long in order to prepare a spiritual bride who will reign with Him in the age to come. The preparation of this bride is the special work of the Spirit in this age.

The fruit of the Spirit is the nature of Christ that is imparted to us through the Spirit. The ministries and gifts of the Spirit are the ministry of Christ imparted to us through the Spirit. Through these we not only identify with Him, but are actually joined to Him in His purpose. The prophecies, dreams, and visions, which result of the pouring out of the Spirit, are also ways in which we begin to see with His eyes and speak what is on His heart.

In a most basic way, the age of the Spirit is when the redemption, reconciliation, and restoration of the cross are worked out in those

> He has waited this long in order to prepare a spiritual bride who will reign with Him in the age to come.

who are called, so that in the age to come they can likewise be used to help in the restoration of the rest of mankind, and the earth, from all of the consequences of the Fall. This is nothing less than the rejoining of heaven and earth. This is the reason the Holy Spirit is given to us—to prepare us for our heavenly home so we can help bring heaven back to the earth, so His kingdom might come and His will be done on the earth again just as it is done in heaven.

We will therefore be devoting this year's articles in *The Morning Star Journal* especially to understanding the Holy Spirit and the spiritual realm that we must become increasingly at home in. Our prayer is that these not only help you to discern the Spirit and what He is doing, but also help impart the faith to follow Him more closely so that you more fully abide in and manifest the Lord.

THE GREAT SOCIETY

The Power of New Testament Church Life

Has the Church Been Beheaded?
by Jim Buchan

All Scriptures are New International Version.

We have all been horrified the past few years at the sight of Muslim radicals who have kidnapped and beheaded innocent civilians in Iraq and other Middle Eastern countries. How could people become so deranged?

But as Christians, there is a beheading which is even more horrifying to consider: Has Christ been removed as the Head of the church?

Of course, in the Father's eyes, Jesus will *always* be the Head of the church, no matter how much we mess things up. Yet I am talking about a more practical issue of Headship. Is Jesus really allowed to be *in charge* of things in most churches? Is He truly the LORD of the church, or just a distant memory that we pay lip-service to?

Maybe we have forgotten what it looks like to have Jesus as the true and living Head of His body. This is not supposed to just be a theoretical or doctrinal position—it is supposed to be REALITY and LIFE.

Take a look at the church in the Book of Acts. It was born in a *prayer meeting* rather than a *board room*. In virtually every chapter in the Book of Acts, we see the church fervently praying and asking the Lord for direction. Without the power and leading of the Holy Spirit, the church would have quickly dissolved. It would have merely had a **"form of godliness but denying its power,"** as Paul warns in II Timothy 3:5.

—In Acts Chapters 1 and 2, the church was born in prayer.
—In Acts Chapters 3-5, miracles were done through prayer.
—In Acts Chapter 6, the church's leaders were ordained with prayer.

—In Acts Chapter 13, the missionaries were directed through prayer.

—In Acts Chapter 15, church issues were resolved in a way that **"seemed good to the Holy Spirit" (verse 28).**

—In Acts Chapter 16, the church in Philippi was planted through prayer.

Jesus was not just a figurehead of His body, He was the REAL Head! While we so cavalierly speak of the "Mission and Vision" of our ministries, the early church had no mission and vision apart from a moment-by-moment reliance on the Holy Spirit!

Moses was warned, **"See to it that you make everything according to the pattern shown you on the mountain" (Hebrews 8:5).** Can we say that we have patterned our church or ministry according to what the Lord showed us during our time with Him "on the mountain?" Or are we merely copycats, taking our pattern from the latest fad or church growth conference?

Although much more could be said on this, let me close with the words of an old worship song:

Jesus, we enthrone You.
We proclaim You are King.
Standing here, in the midst of us,
We lift You up with our praise.
And as we worship, build Your throne.
And as we worship, build Your throne.
And as we worship, build Your throne.
Come, Lord Jesus, and take Your place!

May that be our earnest prayer: Come, Lord Jesus, and take Your place as the rightful Head of Your body! ∎

With more than thirty years of ministry and writing experience, **Jim Buchan** has a passion to equip Christians for greater fruitfulness. He has served as an attorney, pastor, church consultant, conference speaker, and the managing editor of *Ministries Today, Inspiration Today,* and *The Morning Star Journal.* Jim has written several books, including *Walking the Leadership Highway— Without Becoming Roadkill!, Apostolic Evangelism,* and *Taking Your Church's Vital Signs.* For more information about Jim's ministry, contact him at buchanJ@aol.com or 704-770-5200.

WORLD CHANGERS

Past and Present True, Action Heroes

The Victorious Life of Harriet Tubman

by Deborah Joyner Johnson

Trials are a part of life, and the way we deal with them will determine whether we lead a life of victory or defeat. But no matter what the trial is, the Lord will give us power, even in the darkest of times, through the Holy Spirit to overcome, as Acts 1:8 tells us: **"but you shall receive power when the Holy Spirit has come upon you...."**

We have this accessible help all of the time. We can count on the Holy Spirit to lead and guide us. **"But the Helper, the Holy Spirit, whom the Father will send in My name, He will teach you all things, and bring to your remembrance all that I said to you" (John 14:26).** If we will take the time to ask the Lord what to do and say, He will teach us by giving us the answer of how to overcome. He is a ready Teacher; we just have to be ready listeners and doers.

AN AMAZING WOMAN

Harriet Tubman was a woman who faced extreme trials in her life and prevailed against all odds. She knew her purpose and she did not stop until it was accomplished. Throughout her life, Harriet's faith was child-like, her focus remained on the Lord, and she always believed that God would see her through to victory.

We, too, must keep pressing on, just as Harriet Tubman and numerous others have done, who successfully finished the course laid before them. She relied on the power of the Holy Spirit to accomplish so much in her life, and we have the wonderful opportunity to do the same.

Harriet Tubman became the most famous and courageous leader of the Underground Railroad, which gave aid to slaves in the South to escape to the free states.

BORN A SLAVE

Harriet Tubman, an African-American woman, was born into slavery in 1820 in Bucktown, Maryland. Being a slave was one of the most hopeless situations a human could endure, having no rights, very few privileges, and no freedom. Though many slaves had families, any member of their family could be taken and sold at any time, and they would not even know where they went or if they would ever see them again. Think of the pain these families had to suffer.

Though not all slave owners were cruel to their slaves, and some did try to keep families together, treating them with kindness, there were many owners who daily abused their slaves. Harriet was a slave to the latter kind of owners. But perhaps this is just what it took (having suffered so much) to inspire her to want to help others. She did not waste her trials, but learned from them, so she could in turn help others to escape to freedom.

During her time as a slave, Harriet was beaten numerous times on her back and neck, leaving many scars.

Harriet had a loving mother, father, five brothers, and six sisters, but her time of being a child ended at age five when she was forced to work in the fields. During her time as a slave, Harriet was beaten numerous times on her back and neck, leaving many scars. She was forced to work in frigid waters looking after her master's muskrat trappings, and became sick from measles and many bouts of bronchitis, which were never treated, causing her voice to become husky.

But those were not the biggest of her trials. When Harriet was thirteen, she attempted to save another slave from being punished, and was struck in the head with a two-pound iron weight. The impact fractured her skull, and left a dent in her head, scarring her for life. Miraculously, her mother prayed and nursed her back to health after several months. However, she did suffer periodic blackouts and sudden sleepiness from that injury for the rest of her life.

Her owner tried to sell her when she had somewhat recovered, but she was considered damaged goods and no one would buy her. When Harriet did recover enough to function, she began to pray that God would help her get rid of slavery. The accident, though a huge trial in her life, actually caused Harriet's faith to grow in the Lord.

She had continuous conversation with the Lord and became very close to Him. She knew that somehow God was going to use her to help free slaves, but she also knew that apart from God helping her, she could do nothing, as she was a slave, poor, illiterate, and a female.

She knew that somehow God was going to use her to help free slaves....

As Harriet's strength began to return, she stayed busy with physical activity. This enabled her to remain alert and not fall asleep so suddenly. When she was able to work in the fields, her father taught her songs and how to stay alive in the woods, both of which would later be very beneficial to her. Harriet grew amazingly strong so her master started to consider her a showpiece. She could cut a half a cord of wood a day, more than most men. She knew this strength was for a purpose, as she would soon discover.

THE DREAMER

Harriet had significant spiritual gifts. She was gifted prophetically and was often given dreams from the Lord about impending dangers or something that was to happen. While she was young, she kept having a dream about a line that seemed to divide slavery from freedom. She did not know anything about the Mason-Dixon line, but that was what she was seeing. In the dream, she kept seeing people from the North calling her Moses and holding out their hands to her, beckoning her to cross the line.

She would also have dreams about wonderful things that were to happen—such as one about herself flying like a bird over mountains and valleys. She also dreamed about many places she would see later in her escape, which gave her great encouragement from the Lord when she saw them. Harriet had a gift of discernment as well. She could tell if people were for her or against her. All these gifts would prove valuable in the time ahead.

In 1849, Harriet knew it was time for her to escape to the North, when she discovered that she was to be sold, along with two of her brothers, to a Georgia slave trader. They made their plan. Early in the morning Harriet and her two brothers wandered rather idly past the slave quarters and even her master's gate, while singing a song about going to the Promised Land. No one thought it strange, as she seemed to sing much of the time. Her friends could read between the lines though and knew from her song that Harriet was escaping. When her brothers realized the terrible risks that were ahead of them, they returned home and left Harriet alone. She said, "I ain't got no friend but You. Come to my help, Lord, for I'm in trouble." And He did. Harriet knew God so well that she had no doubt He would help her.

Everything was against her. Harriet had no money or map, just a small snack from home, and she was now a hunted fugitive. She had heard blacks could live free in Philadelphia or New York, so she decided to escape to one of those cities.

Harriet began her long travel to the North that night along the Choptank River.

Providentially, Harriet had previously met a Quaker woman in the field close to home, who had offered to help her if she ever decided to escape slavery. This woman was the only one in the world that Harriet knew might help her, so she went there on her first day of escape. Through this woman, Harriet learned about those who could help her through a system of escape called the Underground Railroad. Railroad terminology was used as code words to describe ways of escape, but there was no real railroad. Basically, it consisted of many people using far-reaching signals and codes that helped slaves to escape to the North.

Harriet began her long travel to the North that night along the Choptank River. She followed the North Star when it was in sight, and during cloudy nights, she would feel for moss that grew on the north side of the trees. The Quaker woman gave her directions to a couple's house, where she arrived in the morning. They immediately gave her a broom to work. Harriet wondered if she had been tricked, but this was just part of the plan. Later that day, the man signaled her to get in the wagon of produce and scoot down low under the blankets. He safely took her to the next destination. This was the beginning of being sent to different people and places for food through the help of the Underground Railroad. She traveled at night, staying off main roads. Finally, she had made it past one state line. Fear had tried to grip her, but she kept her eyes on Jesus, knowing He would keep her safe.

At her stop in Wilmington, Delaware, she met Thomas Garrett, a Quaker shoe salesman, who would later become a fearless partner with Harriet in rescuing slaves. He gave escaping slaves food, money, and shoes. At one point, he was fined so heavily for assisting slaves that he lost everything, but that did not stop him. He still kept helping slaves. It is estimated that Garrett helped with the rescue of between 2,500 and 3,000 slaves.

She was determined to help all blacks be free, as she was amazed how wonderful it was to choose where she worked and lived.

Through many dangers and narrow escapes, sleeping in haystacks, storage holes for potatoes, and attics, Harriet finally made it across the Pennsylvania line. The following was her first impression of freedom. "I looked at my hands to see if I was the same person, now that I was free. There was such a glory over everything. The sun came up like gold through the trees and over the fields, and I felt like I was in heaven." Harriet was one of approximately 100,000 slaves who escaped to freedom in the North.

Harriet found places to live and work through the kindness of a man named William Still. In 1850, Congress passed the Fugitive Slave Act, making it illegal to help a runaway slave. That was when Harriet decided to join the Underground Railroad because this was where she felt she could be the most help. She was determined to help all blacks be free, as she was amazed how wonderful it was to choose where she worked and lived. She saved most of her wages by living frugally to help with the purpose of freeing slaves.

From the time she began helping slaves to escape in 1851, which included her own parents and family, she personally helped close to three hundred slaves escape to freedom. Harriet often used songs to communicate any information the slaves might need. She would not tolerate any complaining, or thoughts of giving up, from the slaves she was trying to help to freedom. She was known as "Moses" to her people (just as she was called in her dream) because she helped set many free from the bonds of slavery. She faced danger after danger, but her determination and child-like faith in God enabled her to do what seemed impossible. She listened to the voice of the Holy Spirit many times and was directed away from danger.

One time when she was trying to help a group of slaves escape, her heart began to race, which was always a sign to her that there was danger ahead. It was during winter, and they were on a path deep in the woods near the water. Harriet told everyone to get in the water, and obediently everyone braced for the coldness that would shock their bodies. She said later she felt like the Israelites escaping from the Egyptians when they hit that water. It never went above their heads, and as they proceeded in the water, it became shallower. Later, she learned that just ahead was a group of officers who were looking for her and the runaway slaves. They escaped because Harriet paid attention to the Lord and His warnings.

When she heard the Lord tell her to do something, she did it, without question.

Another time Harriet needed twenty dollars to aid in the escape of her parents. The Lord had told her to go to New York to get the money from a certain man. She told some friends she was going to this man's office and was not leaving until she got the money. When she told the man she needed twenty dollars, he said she was mistaken, that he wasn't giving her twenty dollars. She told him: "The Lord's never been mistaken. Anyhow, I'm going to sit here until I get it!" She did and he gave it to her. That was the kind of determination that Harriet had. When she heard the Lord tell her to do something, she did it, without question.

In another effort to help others escape slavery, Harriet was helping a group to a boat she had planned to take, but had learned it was disabled. They were directed to take another boat, but the clerk would not give her tickets because she did not have a note about being on her master's business or free papers. He told her to stand to the side until he could deal with her. Harriet took a girl named Tilly to the bow of the boat and began praying. Tilly saw the clerk approaching them and feared they were doomed. Harriet pleaded before the Lord to help them until the man reached them. To their astonishment, the clerk told those who were seeking their freedom that they could come and get their tickets. Harriet was not surprised. She knew it was the Lord who had come to their rescue again.

At one point, a reward of $40,000 was offered for her capture. Harriet would often get someone to follow those who were putting up "wanted" signs for her and other runaway slaves and tear them down. The slave drivers caught up to her one time, when suddenly she had one of her blackouts. They never saw her as she lay sleeping in the field. God had protected her once again. During the many times she aided slaves to freedom, she was never caught, nor did she lose a slave to the Southern militia, as the Lord guarded her every step. Her life embodied the biblical principle in Zechariah 4:6: **"'Not by might nor by power, but by My Spirit,' says the Lord."**

It was Harriet's deep faith in God that not only sustained her, but propelled her to a lifelong service to Him and His people.

It was not enough for Harriet to just lead others to freedom from their Egypt; she wanted them to be established in their new Promised Land. She helped them find work and places to live once they were free. During the Civil War, Harriet served as a nurse, scout, and sometimes as a spy for the Union army. After the war, Harriet established a rest home for the poor and elderly. Throughout her life, she helped others to experience true freedom.

Harriet died at the life-fulfilled age of ninety-three. Her life was truly remarkable. No obstacle stopped Harriet from achieving her goal of freeing slaves. It was Harriet's deep faith in God that not only sustained her, but propelled her to a lifelong service to Him and His people. When she heard the Holy Spirit speak, she acted. Fear did not grip her because she gave her anxiety to the Lord. She never doubted that He would be with her.

Amazingly, she was never bitter toward those who hurt her or persecuted her. She chose to forgive and pray for those who mistreated her.

Harriet's goal was to bring African-Americans and whites together in unity. Even through such a life of trials, she remained cheerful. Life held joy. She brought hope to others through joyful songs and would sing many times, "I'm going to hold steady on You!" She truly did.

JUST BELIEVE

God will never ask us to do something that we are not capable of doing. He will prepare us in every way. However, it will take a tremendous amount of faith to walk in the type of calling Harriet Tubman had. For those who believe, all things are possible through God. He will give strength to accomplish the extraordinary.

The trials that we face can become victories on our road to Him, if we choose to overcome them. The Lord speaks in many ways, and those who know Him will hear His voice. He is a sure Guide and Helper. Just as He faithfully helped Harriet Tubman, He will do the same for us. Just believe.

We are now in need of many like her who will help lead their brethren to spiritual freedom, resolving to continue until all are free of the yoke of bondage to sin and evil. We, likewise, need a spiritual "Underground Railroad" that will aid in every way and provide what is needed for those who are risking all in pursuit of the true liberty of the Spirit.

Now may the God of hope fill you with all joy and peace in believing, that you may abound in hope by the power of the Holy Spirit (Romans 15:13). ■

The material for this article was taken from Harriet Tubman, by Rebecca Price Janney, Bethany House Publishers.

Deborah Joyner Johnson is the managing editor for MorningStar Publications and Ministries. Deborah writes articles for *The Morning Star Journal* and has published two books, *The Chosen Path* and *Pathway to Purpose*. She has a gifted teaching ministry and shares at conferences and women's groups. Deborah lives in North Carolina and has three children: Matthew, Meredith, and Abby.

PROPHETIC PERSPECTIVES

Seeing Tomorrow Today, and How We Can Be Prepared For It

A Recipe for Disaster

by Rick Joyner

The prayer that the Lord gave His people to pray was for His kingdom to come and His will to be done on earth as it is in heaven (see Matthew 6:10). Having been probably prayed by every Christian in history, we can be sure that this prayer will be answered. The kingdom is going to come, and no utopian philosophy has even proposed just how wonderful this world will actually be when it does. Of course, the great question is, when?

The Lord assured His disciples that no man could know the day or hour in which He would return, but the Scriptures are clear that we can have a part in determining when it will take place, such as II Peter 3:12, which says that we should be **"looking for and hastening the coming of the day of God...."** In light of this, an even more important question would be: How can we hasten the coming of the Lord?

The Lord also said that He could not return until the gospel of the kingdom was preached throughout the world as a witness (see Matthew 24:14). The gospel of the kingdom has probably not been preached since the first century. We have preached the gospel of salvation, the gospel of the church, and the gospel of many truths, all of which are wonderful, but they are not the gospel of the kingdom. The gospel of the kingdom is the good news about His kingdom coming to the earth so that God's will is done on earth just as it is in heaven.

The good news about the coming of the kingdom is much better than the news that the church has been focused on for decades now, which is that the end of the world is near. It is the end of this age, and this age will end with a time of trouble such as the world has never seen, but that is not the gospel. The gospel is that this age of darkness, rebellion, and war is just about over, and the King is coming to make all things right. We cannot continue to allow the new age movements and all of the cults and false religions to seize the high ground of hope for the future when the church has been given the greatest hope of all.

The great tribulation, the antichrist, the prophesied wars, earthquakes, famines, and other problems are issues that should be understood, but they are not the main issues we should be focused on. If we are really going to understand the times, we should spend far more time on seeing and being a part of what Christ is doing than trying to understand what the antichrist is doing.

One main thing that Christ is doing right now is preparing His people to preach the gospel of the kingdom, to refocus us more on the Great Commission than the Great Tribulation. The gospel of the kingdom will soon be preached with power and authority to demonstrate the power and authority of the coming kingdom. The world will have a witness that the authority and power of the kingdom of God will prevail over all earthly kingdoms and will soon come to the earth so that God's will is done here just as it is in heaven.

> **We also know from the prophecies of Scripture that the end of this age will be the greatest time of trouble the world has ever known.**

We also know from the prophecies of Scripture that the end of this age will be the greatest time of trouble the world has ever known. We do not want to overlook these, but rather understand them so that we can be prepared for them. However, the best way to be prepared for them is to see and enter the kingdom, which we can do now. The kingdom of God is a kingdom that cannot be shaken, and when the entire world is shaking, those who have built their lives on the kingdom will be as steady as a rock because they are standing on the Rock.

You have to be born again to see the kingdom. You have to use the keys of the kingdom to enter it. The main key to the kingdom is to "**...seek first His kingdom and His righteousness...**" (**Matthew 6:33**). To seek His kingdom first is to make all major decisions based on the interests of the kingdom. Many Christians have lived fruitless lives of frustration because they made the decision on where they would live based on where the best job opportunity was, or where the best geography was, or family—or just about anything other than the interests of the kingdom. The Lord will still be with us when we do this, and will bless us and take care of us as much as He can, but we will not be in His will.

A huge repositioning has been going on for a time and will continue as many Christians wake up to the fact that they are not in God's will geographically. If our identity is mostly in what we do in the secular realm, such as being an engineer, doctor, or school teacher, rather than who we are in Christ, then we have sought our secular position in this world more than we have sought our position in the body of Christ. Do we live where we are because it is where the best job is or because it is where the Lord has placed us in His body, the church?

> **We cannot be properly joined to the Head without also being properly joined to His body.**

Presently, most Christians have a church life that is somewhere between frustrating and non-existent. These mostly tend to blame the church for being in such bad shape, but the main reason for this is that they are not in the right place and will never fit well into the church in their region. We are told in I Corinthians 11:29-30, **"For he who eats and drinks, eats and drinks judgment to himself, if he does not judge the body rightly. For this reason many among you are weak and sick, and a number sleep."** This is still true; most of the weakness, sickness, and premature death among Christians is the result of not discerning the body rightly, and therefore not fitting into it.

We cannot be properly joined to the Head without also being properly joined to His body. His life blood flows through His body, which is why we are told in I John 1:7, **"but if we walk in the light as He Himself is in the light, we have fellowship with one another, and the blood of Jesus His Son cleanses us from all sin."** The true fellowship of the Spirit that can only be found in an authentic church relationship and is required for walking in the light and for His life blood to flow through us.

The word that is translated **"fellowship"** throughout the New Testament, including these texts quoted above, is the Greek word *koinonia* which means much more than a slap on the back and handshake on Sunday mornings. It is a deep and vital interconnection and relationship like organs are connected to a body. If you disconnect the organ it will die fast. If it is a vital organ the whole body will die as well.

The most important thing that we can do to be prepared for the times is to get close to the Lord and to find our right place in His body. This is the first step in seeking His kingdom first. We can know all of the prophetic scenarios accurately, but will still be in grave danger if we have not been obedient to this command.

TROUBLES ARE DOORWAYS

In Acts 14:22, we are told that **"through many tribulations we must enter the kingdom of God."** This is basically because troubles compel us to find the Lord, who is the answer to every human problem. In the same way, the Great Tribulation will be the doorway through which the whole world enters the kingdom.

The Great Tribulation is basically the result of mankind trying to run this world without God. We are fast entering the time when human wisdom, power, and resources will not be able to cope with the magnitude of the problems arising in the world. However, there

> As the troubles in the world increase, the light and power that is revealed through the church will grow.

is wisdom, power, and resources to deal with any human problem. Jesus Christ, His atonement, and the provision for His reconciliation to the world so that His kingdom can come are the answers to every human problem. We are going to begin to see this demonstrated repeatedly, and in every place.

As the troubles in the world increase, the light and power that is revealed through the church will grow. The church will start to be esteemed as the source of the greatest wisdom, power, and resources for the great and increasing needs of the world. This is how Jesus preached the gospel of the kingdom, by demonstrating its power and authority over any condition on the earth. There are no cripples or blind people in heaven, so He demonstrated what would happen when the power of the kingdom of heaven touched a cripple or blind person on the earth. There is no lack for anything in heaven, so He demonstrated what would happen when heaven touched the need for wine at a wedding, or to feed thousands of hungry people, even multiplying the lunch of a little boy with a single touch and blessing from above.

The resources of heaven cannot be exhausted. If they were used to pay off all of the debts of every nation and every individual on earth, heaven would not even know anything was missing. This is the primary job of the church in the last days of this age—to witness and demonstrate the power of the kingdom over any condition on the earth. To do this, we must be living in the kingdom ourselves. The gospel of the kingdom will therefore need to be preached to the church first, and the church must choose to build on the kingdom of heaven and not the kingdoms of this world. This will be a practical, step-by-step process, but it will not take long. The shaking that is coming upon the world—to shake everything that can be shaken, is beginning to happen, and Christians are starting to flee to the kingdom instead of just wistfully dreaming about it.

> **When we begin to see who Jesus really is, we will see the heavens opened....**

JACOB'S LADDER

When Jesus told Nathanael that He saw him under the fig tree, Nathanael was so astonished that he immediately declared Jesus to be the Christ, the Son of God. The Lord replied to him, **"'Because I said to you that I saw you under the fig tree, do you believe? You shall see greater things than these.' And He said to him, 'Truly, truly, I say to you, you shall see the heavens opened, and the angels of God ascending and descending on the Son of Man'" (John 1:50-51).** When we begin to see who Jesus really is, we will see the heavens opened and the messengers of God will ascend into heaven upon Him, returning to the earth with evidence of heaven's reality. This is our most basic calling. The door to heaven is opened by this one thing—seeing who Jesus really is, where He sits above all authority, power, and dominion. The true understanding of the kingdom is first and foremost a true understanding of who Jesus is.

I Corinthians 1:24 declares "**...Christ the power of God and the wisdom of God.**" As we begin to see Him as He is and He begins to take His rightful place as the Head of the church, the church is going to be filled with Him, His power, and His wisdom. The gift of the Spirit that is about to take preeminence for a time is the gift of "a word of wisdom," which is supernatural wisdom from above. This will come forth through the church with such profound power, which cannot be disputed or confounded. We are about to see the government of God, the kingdom of God, revealed as the only source of light and power that can confront and overcome the great darkness of the time. Again, Jesus Christ is the answer to every human problem. The church is going to learn this and then the world is going to see it through the church.

Disasters have been with the world since the Fall and will continue until the King returns. There are many which can be avoided by prayer and/or repentance. These we need to avoid. There are others that will not be avoided. These we must use for good. Everything that is meant for evil can be turned into a victory for the kingdom.

> **The church that is about to arise will have the resolve to see the Lord glorified in every situation....**

The church that is about to arise will have the resolve to see the Lord glorified in every situation; even the worst human disasters will be turned into good. We must not settle for anything less than the victory of the kingdom over evil, regardless of how bad the disaster or problem is. In fact, the worse the disaster, or the greater the problem, the greater the opportunity to do good and rebuild what was lost on a foundation that cannot be shaken.

THE CLEANSING OF KATRINA

The very word Katrina means to cleanse or make clean. That will be the ultimate result of this storm. The Gulf Coast that was hit by this mega storm is still in a state of almost unimaginable devastation and depression. Even though the refuse of the storm has been mostly cleaned up, the emptiness is palpable. That will change. It will be turned into good, and the same region will be the source of one of the great revivals in history. It will be a spiritual jubilee, setting many captives free.

However, we must learn the lessons of Katrina. As Francis Frangipane likes to say, "You never fail one of God's tests—you just keep taking them until you pass." We don't want to take any more tests like this than we have to, so let's resolve to pass this test by gaining all of the understanding that we can from it, making the necessary changes needed so that no more such disasters are necessary.

You never fail one of God's tests—you just keep taking them until you pass.

Can we get to a place where no more disasters are necessary? Absolutely. There will be cities of refuge through all that is coming, safe zones where Psalm 91 has been applied. These can be cities or nations. The Lord would much rather show mercy than judgment, but if He has to, for our sake, He will send judgment. We actually choose if we need it or how severe it will be through our response to His warnings.

As devastating as Katrina was, it was just a warning. It could have been much, much worse. We now know that Katrina came ashore as a Level 3 storm. How devastating would it have been if it had hit at its peak power as a Level 5? How much more deadly would it have been if the levies had broken during the storm when people would not have been able to escape from the floodwaters and get on their roofs? Make no mistake about it; God did remember mercy with Katrina. Did we get the message, or will it take more?

Hurricane Katrina brought out the best and the worst in our nation. In many ways, it was a revelation of the true state of the nation. It is crucial that we, the church, who are called to be the light and salt of the earth, understand this revelation in order to be prepared for the times and proactive in the midst of them. The church was without question one of the brightest lights in response to the Katrina disaster—a fact that was even admitted to by the liberal press. In the time to come, she will shine brighter and brighter.

The evaluations of the situation and problems, which were cast about during the disaster were revealing, but in the stress and emotion of the catastrophe, they were not very accurate. However, now that we have had more than a year to consider this disaster, the revelations of our strengths and weaknesses are much more dependable, and the lessons can be much more helpful. We must learn these lessons because the church will have an increasing role to play in future disasters, and now is the time to prepare for them.

As great as the response of the church was in the Katrina disaster, it can be many times more effective if we plan and prepare now for what the Scriptures make clear will be coming. There will be more storms, earthquakes, floods, famines, and as lawlessness increases, devastating terrorist and criminal attacks. If we believe that we will be raptured out before the Great Tribulation, we need to understand that all of these things were prophesied to come as **"the beginning of birth pangs" (see Matthew 24:8).** Even if the church is taken out before the Great Tribulation, being prepared for times of trouble is still wise. Our main preparation for them is to simply obey and abide in the Lord and use these times to preach His gospel.

> **T**hose who are adequately prepared for the times will not fear the times.

If fear rises in you at just the mention of these things, know that your fear can be easily expelled. I have watched many who were gripped by fear of such things become bold and proactive in the midst of them with just a little training and preparation. Those who are adequately prepared for the times will not fear the times.

THE COMING GREAT THEOLOGICAL SHIFT

Some Christians see nothing but bad times coming. Others cannot see anything bad coming because they have faith that it won't. Both extremes are inaccurate and thankfully most Christians have a much more balanced, biblical view of the future. One of the most clear prophecies is Isaiah 60:1-5:

"Arise, shine; for your light has come, and the glory of the Lord has risen upon you.

"For behold, darkness will cover the earth, and deep darkness the peoples, but the LORD will rise upon you, and His glory will appear upon you.

"And nations will come to your light, and kings to the brightness of your rising.

"Lift up your eyes round about, and see; they all gather together, they come to you. Your sons will come from afar, and your daughters will be carried in the arms.

"Then you will see and be radiant, and your heart will thrill and rejoice; because the abundance of the sea will be turned to you, the wealth of the nations will come to you."

> Christians in all extremes are moving toward one another, and a great unity is going to start taking form in the church.

At the very time darkness is covering the earth and deep darkness the people, the Lord's glory will arise on His people. The result of this will be the nations turning to God's people, even bringing their wealth. This promise is for natural Zion, Israel, and spiritual Zion, the church. So, as some things start to get darker, we should begin looking for more glory. These are the times that the prophets of old desired to see, and we have been chosen to live in them!

Most Christians wander off into some theological extremes from time to time, realize they are off course, get back on the path of life, and keep moving. There is a ditch on either side of the path of life, and sometimes coming out of one, we overreact and fall into the ditch on the other side. However, most, if they just keep moving, stop drifting to extremes and learn to stay on the path. As remarkable as this may seem, Christians in all extremes are moving toward one another, and a great unity is going to start taking form in the church.

As we get closer to the end of this age, there will be increasing troubles in the world. Even so, "**...we know that God causes all things to work together for good to those who love God, to those who are called according to His purpose" (Romans 8:28).** For those who have built their lives on the kingdom which cannot be shaken, it really does not matter what happens in the world because they will not be moved, except with compassion to help those who are in need. Those who are prepared will have faith, not fear. They will not suffer loss, but rather reap a harvest.

Disaster response is going to be one of the most important and effective ministries in the time to come and will be a primary vehicle for turning the people who are in darkness to the light of the Lord. There will be more storms, earthquakes, floods, fires, terrorist attacks, and criminal acts that cause great devastation. However, the worst tribulation our neighbors may ever know could come at the next stoplight. To be trained and prepared for disaster response is to be quick and proactive at responding to disasters, big or small. Not only is a great harvest going to come from this, but the esteem of the church in the eyes of the world is going to rise dramatically because of it.

This ministry of helps that arises within the church is also going to help the church more than any other ministry project in history.

Almost nothing makes friends faster and deeper than helping someone in their time of need. The Holy Spirit is the Helper, and if we really are Spirit-filled, Spirit-led people, we will be there for our neighbors to help in their time of need. This is the true ministry of "helps," to be able and willing to respond to those who cry "Help!" Even some of the most radical Muslims in the world started to esteem Christians in a whole new way after the tsunami disaster in Indonesia because of the way they were helped by Christian relief agencies. When someone helps you or your family through a crisis, there is an appreciation and often a bonding that goes deeper than could ever happen otherwise.

This ministry of helps that arises within the church is also going to help the church more than any other ministry project in history. It will mobilize and energize the lives of Christians like few things have ever done before. There is a fulfillment and satisfaction that comes from helping others in a desperate time of need that can change the life of the one who helps as well. This will begin to deliver many believers from the spiritual apathy and lukewarmness that have gripped them. Souls will be saved, and teachers and pastors will be raised up to take care of them and establish them on a solid foundation. Churches will swell in number so fast that it is going to be extremely hard to keep up with the growth.

WHERE ARE WE?

When you go into a shopping mall, at most entrances they have a map of the mall which shows the location of the different stores. However, this map would be useless in finding the location of the store if it did not have the little dot that says, "You are here." Once you know where you are, it is easy to determine the best way to get to where you want to go. However, knowing where you are is not very helpful if you do not know where you are going. We need to know both where we are and where we are going.

> Churches will swell in number so fast that it is going to be extremely hard to keep up with the growth.

We must keep in mind that the Great Commission is to make disciples of nations, not just individuals. God is going to be dealing more and more with nations as His kingdom approaches. The Katrina disaster showed us much about where we are as a nation. We need to evaluate this and understand it as fully as we can to use it to get to where we are supposed to be.

The prophecies of Scripture are clear about where we are going in general, and prophetic gifts are given for more specific guidance. We need to grow in our understanding of the prophecies of Scripture and promote the growth of the proven prophetic gifts the church has been given. These prophetic gifts are some of the divinely powerful weapons we have been given. They are "weapons of mass construction" which are given to help build the kingdom.

Many prophetic people had foreseen the coming of Hurricane Katrina. However, I do not know a single church or ministry that was prepared for it when it hit. This we must acknowledge and learn from. The devil had his people prepared. Just days after the storm, they were at city hall with a plan for rebuilding the city which they had been working on for years. In Biloxi, it was a plan for basically letting the casinos and their associated businesses take over. I was told that the mayor asked one of our relief workers why the church did not have something like this. We should have.

The good will and appreciation for the church and Christians after Katrina was so great we could have won the battle for the future of that town if we had been prepared with a plan for it, but we were not. The casino owners were prepared and took advantage of the vacuum. They won that round, but we do not have to lose the next one. We must take the foreknowledge we are given and use it to plan strategically for the future.

A BEAUTIFUL MIND

There has been a knee-jerk reaction to planning among many Pentecostals and Charismatics, considering that anything planned by man could not be from the Holy Spirit. Nothing could be further from the truth or sound biblical teaching. We are called to be conformed to the image of Christ, and it is His plan by which we are all saved, and by which the earth and all it contains will be restored. Planning is a very basic nature of God and sound planning should be our basic nature as well. Of course, we do not want carnal planning from carnally minded men, but spiritual planning from those who have had their minds renewed and transformed so that they have the mind of Christ. This renewed and powerful mind is also a gift from God.

The whole world is going to soon start taking note of the astonishing and profound wisdom that comes through the church. The plans and wisdom with which the church moves, builds, and does what we are called to do will start getting the attention of the world. As Christians begin to become properly aligned with Christ and His body, their minds will not be as clouded with the lusts or the fears of this world, and clarity will come to them that is greater than they have ever known.

A NEW WAVE OF THE PROPHETIC

We are told in Acts 2:17-21 that in **"the last days"** the Holy Spirit will be poured out. The result of this is that prophecy, dreams, and visions are released to male and female, old and young, which means everyone. This increasing prophetic revelation at the end of the age is coming because we are going to need it for the times.

The Lord chastised the people for being able to discern the signs of the weather better than they could discern the signs of the times. The Lord always used metaphors that were related, and discerning the weather is a lot like discerning the times. In the last few decades, weather forecasting has gone from being a joke and ridiculed to being amazingly accurate and getting more so all of the time. However, many people continue to think of weather forecasting the way it was rather than the way it now is. The same has been true with the emerging prophetic ministry.

> **P**opularity can be one of the hardest of all trials for the prophetic.

As a pilot, my life could depend on accurate weather forecasting. The same is true for those who make their living on the sea. In the time to come, we will find our lives increasingly dependent on accurate, dependable prophetic ministry. We must continue to devote ourselves to seeing this ministry mature and take its rightful place among the ministries of the church. Without prophetic ministry, the church will continue to stumble into the future blind and vulnerable.

In the last few decades, like weather forecasting, the prophetic ministry has made strides forward in its accuracy and dependability. However, many seem to think of it as still being in the immature state that it was two or three decades ago, but this is to be expected.

The ridicule and outright persecution of the prophetic ministry by other Christians has actually helped the prophetic a lot by driving away the many pseudo prophets who were drawn to it when it was popular, but were the ones creating much of the confusion. As the prophetic becomes not only popular again, but is also seen as increasingly essential, we need to recognize and watch out for the pretenders who will try to associate with the prophetic this time. They will do much damage, and as we see throughout the Scriptures, it is the job of the prophetic ministry to deal with the false prophets. Popularity can be one of the hardest of all trials for the prophetic.

During the time when many were rejecting prophetic ministry, some of the world's most powerful leaders in government, business, sports, and even the military, began to think more highly of the prophetic ministry given to the church than the church did. The prophetic has been used to help them, sometimes in spectacular ways. However, we must never forget that this ministry is first for the church.

In many ways, rejection is essential for the healthy development of authentic prophetic ministry, which must not be overly concerned by what people think in order to do what they are called to do. Even so, the mature prophetic ministries will be like Christ, not rejecting in return, but laying down their lives even for the ones who rejected them.

> **R**ejection is essential for the healthy development of authentic prophetic ministry, which must not be overly concerned by what people think....

The prophets in Scripture were often called watchmen because they were spiritually positioned like watchmen on the walls, able to see what was coming from afar. There are dependable watchmen with extraordinary gifts being raised up today. Before the end of this age comes, every local church will have its own recognized and credible watchmen on the walls. Others will be watchmen for whole cities, nations, and such things as corporations and industries, which is already happening to some degree.

In biblical times, the watchmen of a city were positioned on the walls, and they conveyed what they saw to the elders who sat in the gates, who determined what action needed to be taken based on this information. They could sound the alarm when an enemy or thieves were coming. They could likewise command the gates to be opened for merchants with important resources for the city. This partnership between the watchmen and elders is now being established in many churches, and in other realms such as governments, industries, etc. Not having this relationship will prove increasingly costly in the time to come.

The Lord is not giving the prophetic revelation that is described in Acts 2 just for our entertainment or to make our meetings more exciting. We are going to need it to survive the times, but we are called to do much more than that—we are called to seize the times, preaching the gospel of the coming kingdom of God, and in places taking spiritual dominion over our cites and regions in preparation for this.

WHERE WE ARE GOING

The whole nation, and even much of the world, was traumatized by mismanagement during the Katrina disaster. The wealthiest, most powerful nation on earth was brought to its knees by a single storm. This will increasingly be the case in almost every realm from politics to natural disasters to medicine—the problems we are facing are beyond human remedy. As stated, the "great time of trouble" prophesied to come at the end is basically the result of mankind trying to run the world without God, and reaping the foolishness that has been sown because of this. Even so, in truth the response to Hurricane Katrina was not as bad as the media made it seem, but it was bad.

> The whole nation, and even much of the world, was traumatized by mismanagement during the Katrina disaster.

As is usually the case, the ones who did the most accusing and blame-shifting during this disaster were probably the most guilty of mismanagement. This is almost always the case. We must start to more quickly discern that the people who do the most criticizing in such things are usually trying to hide their own failures. This was the case with the Hurricane Katrina disaster. Many did needlessly die, not because the resources were not available, but because they were not managed properly. That can be, and needs to be, fixed. However, to do this we need to understand the mismanagement, not for the sake of accusing anyone, but in order to fix the problem.

I once heard how an executive cost his company hundreds of thousands of dollars by a foolish decision. When the owner was asked if he was going to fire this man his reply was, "Of course not! I just spent hundreds of thousands of dollars educating him. Why would I fire him and give him to my competitors?" The point is that some who make the greatest mistakes, as we see in Scripture, can, if they learn from them, be used to do great things. Likewise, those who have humbled themselves by admitting their mistakes in this disaster should not be thrown away. Most of the key people involved in the Federal government, including the President, did this—they humbled themselves and admitted the mistakes.

The mismanagement of resources during this storm was not just on the part of FEMA, but the local governments were just as bad, and possibly worse. We heard over and over how the poor in New Orleans could not afford the transportation to evacuate before the storm, but then we saw the hundreds of school buses that sat idle that could have easily done the job. To do this required planning and proactive leadership both of which seemed to be absent, even though the city and state had many years to prepare for this disaster.

There is a list too long to examine in detail of other major mismanagement problems that exacerbated the already tragic situation after Hurricane Katrina. However, we should keep in mind that most of our elected officials are not elected for their crisis management ability, and most have little or no experience in it. The qualities that can make one a good leader in times of peace can make them a very bad leader in times of crisis. Leadership and management in crisis situations is a very unique and rare gift. However, for the time to come this needs to be one of the basic qualities we look for in our leaders.

> Just a little bit of planning and preparation now can save many in the time to come.

Government officials on all levels are increasingly burdened by a continuous onslaught of minor crises to the extent that they often have little time to consider or prepare for major ones. To remedy this, many government leaders and managers are being required to go through some crisis management training to know their available resources, and how to mobilize and use them when needed. This is a positive step, and it should be done with every church leader as well.

RESOURCES ARE AVAILABLE

Just a little bit of planning and preparation now can save many in the time to come. There is some basic training that every pastor and church leader should take. The chaplain's training provided by the International Fellowship of Chaplains (IFOC) is excellent, and is now being made widely available to the church. So is the Crisis Intervention and Stress

Management (CISM) training offered by FEMA. Our leadership team went through these and immediately we could see how everyone in any ministry could benefit greatly from them even if they never worked in a major disaster.

The credentials provided by completing these courses can also open major doors for ministry and will most likely raise your church's esteem in the eyes of the local officials. That esteem can give you access to other powerful ministry opportunities and help make your church a true light to your community. It is no accident that church buildings are called "sanctuaries." The church is going to become the sanctuary from the storms that are coming. We need to be prepared for this.

Trauma is one of the devil's primary inroads into a person's life.

Just one example of how this training can be helpful was demonstrated by one of our local church elder's wives that went through the chaplain's training. Immediately after she finished the course, the husband of the family next door to her committed suicide. By her own admission, if she had not had this training she would not have known what to do to help. However, because she was armed with the training, she became proactive and engaged, leading that devastated family to the Help they needed. What could have terribly damaged their lives left no bad effects, but rather a victory instead.

Few understand that 40 percent of all people who are given a death notice of a loved one react violently, even to the point of going to get a gun to shoot the messenger. This is serious business, and people who have been trained and experienced in this for years can impart wisdom to us in hours. The church needs to take this burden of giving death notices off of its local police forces and turn this most difficult task into ministry to those who mourn. Isn't the Holy Spirit the Comforter? No one will ever be able to do this better than one who is anointed by the Spirit, and most police forces will gladly give this difficult task to those who will take it.

Trauma is one of the devil's primary inroads into a person's life. We need to shut that gate of hell, and learn to use every traumatic situation as an opportunity for the Lord, the Comforter, the Helper, to prevail in that situation. A large church could be built using the obituary page in the paper to reach out to people in crisis. A sincere sympathy card with a personal note can be such a touch from the Comforter. This is not trying to take advantage of people in a weak state; it is doing our job to serve them in their time of need.

An increasing number who have been through chaplain's training have not only become a huge and trusted resource by their local police force, but some have had major inroads into companies by helping their people through crisis. Others have found a place ministering to sports teams, schools, and other institutions. Once the Helper starts using you, not only will you find a fulfillment and satisfaction that is greater than almost any other accomplishment, but this may be the biggest open door of all to "full time ministry" for those who feel called to this but have never found a way to do it.

Because many local churches do not have the resources to bring this kind of training to their own church, we will be offering these regularly at H.I.M. We can offer them at a fraction of their usual cost because of the numbers we bring in. Also, to do this training together in a setting like Heritage, with people from many other churches, states, and even nations, also enables us to meet and develop relationships with other church leaders who are becoming engaged in this important mission.

> **The media now has a knee-jerk tendency to pick out and highlight the negative and controversial issues....**

TELEVISION UNREALITY

As I alluded to above, the media may have exaggerated some in its coverage of the Katrina disaster mismanagement, but if they did it was at least in part due to them trying very hard to help the nation understand and mobilize for this disaster. Overall, the media did a great job with their coverage of Katrina, and most sincerely were trying to convey a true picture of the disaster. Even so, the media now has a knee-jerk tendency to pick out and highlight the negative and controversial issues, which causes it to sometimes completely miss the positive things that are happening.

When I first visited the disaster area, my first response was shock at the overwhelming destruction which TV just could not possibly convey. It was hard to believe that I was standing on American soil in the midst of such tragedy. My next response was to be overwhelmingly thankful to be an American. It was truly wonderful to see the multitudes of individuals, Christians, Muslims, Jews, and heathens who responded. Companies loaded up their corporate aircraft and began flying in supplies they had either manufactured or purchased to send to the victims. They were not sending junk either. I heard many victims say that they had never had such great clothes, food, or felt such caring from the church, companies, or their government.

> **I**t was truly wonderful to see the multitudes of individuals, Christians, Muslims, Jews, and heathens who responded.

Despite those who were so vocal in their complaints about the government's response, overall our government did a remarkable job facing the obstacles that they did. They may not have made the news, but there were many stories of those who took great comfort in the way their government mobilized, and even if it was inept in some areas that governments will typically be, there was no question that our government cared, was at least trying to help, and did help greatly in many ways. I was sorry that more of these stories of true heroism on the part of many government officials and corporations that mobilized to help were not told.

THE BEST OF TIMES AND WORST OF TIMES

For a time, everyone seemed to be shocked and overwhelmed by the magnitude of the Katrina disaster. The best came to the surface as common people, often with no training or expertise in an area, became proactive in coming up with solutions to overwhelming problems. They may have been imperfect solutions, but most of them were good enough to work—doing anything helped in many cases. Once improvising started it was carried to an art form. The creativity that came out of people in this situation was truly remarkable.

The worst of people also surfaced—the ones who prey on the misfortune of others, or who start blame-shifting and accusing others for their own failures. Almost before the winds stopped, I started getting reports from the first people we sent down that they thought the mayor of New Orleans was going to incite a riot with what he was putting out on the radio. I never heard what he was saying that they thought would cause this, but the problems were exacerbated in a most tragic way. Soon shots were even being fired at the rescue workers, substantially delaying further relief of the people in desperate need.

Then other local leaders stepped up their blame of FEMA and the Federal government for not doing more. It later became obvious that the breakdown on the part of the government was on every level, not just the federal. Then came the accusation that this was all done out of racism. This was the worst thing that could have been said, at the worst time, and with no evidence whatsoever for bringing such a charge. This caused a huge backlash, and actually sowed the seeds of racism more than possibly anything could have. This polarization does have the potential to do much more damage to the country than Katrina.

> **I**t later became obvious that the breakdown on the part of the government was on every level, not just the federal.

Racism, in any form, is one of the ultimate evils of the human heart because it is founded upon two of the greatest evils—fear and pride. We become racist when we are so insecure that we fear those who are not just like us, or when we have the most terrible and profound form of pride—pride in the flesh.

I confess that when I heard the racist charges being made by some black leaders I had to fight a rise in racism in my own heart toward them. Some of these leaders I had come to have a growing respect for, even to the point that when I saw them on the news or a talk show, I would go out of my way to listen to them and consider their points of view. When they came with these charges of racism at such a terrible time, I thought they so irresponsibly overplayed the race card that this would certainly cost them all credibility, and it certainly did cost them a lot.

I do not believe in writing anyone off, especially because of just one mistake, but this was so out of place and so damaging that they will have to do something very remarkable for me to respect them or trust them again. I know I am far from being alone in this disappointment. This irresponsibility caused the rise of racism, and probably set back black leadership in this country many years. As soon as the racism charges were made, others reacted and started saying things like "There weren't any white people shooting at the rescuers." It seemed for a time as if this could cause a meltdown.

Some courageous reporters rose up to call these racism charges baseless and hurtful. This helped a lot. If racism is ever going to be healed, it is going to be on the basis of truth. If we are going to be true, we are going to have to start calling bigotry "bigotry" regardless of who it comes through. The charges of racism on the part of those black leaders was the most racist act in the disaster and did make matters much worse, not better.

If racism is ever going to be healed, it is going to be on the basis of truth.

Even so, we must understand that there is a new order of black leadership rising in America. The old order, which has worn out the racist card to manipulate people, is an archaic and dying breed. There is a new breed of black leadership which is above using such base tactics, and we must be careful not to judge them because of what others are doing. This new breed will rise above being thought of as just black leaders, but will be leaders. All of America, black, white, Hispanic, Asian, Native American, and all other ethnic groups, will be the beneficiaries of the new breed of leadership that is arising from the black community.

America does have a tragic history of racism. Most of it has been white on black crime, and of the most diabolical type. However, now it at least seems that most racist crime is black on white. We can understand how the oppressed black community is still wounded and bitter, but Satan will not cast out Satan, and when we return evil for evil we only multiply evil. There is the potential for a devastating race war in every nation, including America. However, a black leadership is taking its rightful place in almost every field now, including government, and now represents some of the best leadership in America. When someone has the right to be angry or bitter, but rises above it, they have a dignity and class that will cause trust in those of all races. We must not judge all black leadership by the few who seemed to let the worst come out of them during this crisis.

Even so, what surfaced in New Orleans was a revelation of where we are, and we are a long way from overcoming the racism in America. Racism can be expected to raise its head at the worst times in the future if we do not proactively engage and overcome it. America, which is made up of those from every nation, culture, and race, may have the best opportunity to do this of any nation. We must if we are going to survive the times.

A ROOT OF LAWLESSNESS

The prophecies of Scripture make clear that lawlessness will be one of the worst problems at the end of the age. Socialism is one of the biggest roots of lawlessness. Socialism has multitudes of people considering the government as the source for all of their needs, and as governments are increasingly unable to provide them, the rebellion of these people will be quick and vicious.

MorningStar joined Urban Life Ministries to run a POD (point of distribution) in Biloxi, Mississippi after Katrina. We provided three hot meals a day for several thousand and helped distribute clothes, tents, and almost everything else needed by the victims. By Christmas, it was estimated that our base had distributed about 25 million dollars worth of food and other materials to the victims. Our people also worked clearing the downed trees, rubble, removing mold from houses, and just about everything that required physical labor. This was all done by volunteers who were there on their own time, not making anything for what was probably the hardest, most dangerous work they had ever done. The victims that we helped were generally very grateful, but some were demanding to the point of being obnoxious, and a few became enraged if something was not done the way

> **R**acism can be expected to raise its head at the worst times in the future if we do not proactively engage and overcome it.

they wanted, or in the time that they expected it. In most of these cases, and possibly all of them, it was the ones who were on welfare who were the most demanding and obnoxious.

When God created man, He put him in the Garden to cultivate it. Man was created first to have a relationship with God, but we were also created to work. Studies have shown that those who are deprived of meaningful labor will go insane. There is a basic need in every human being to accomplish something. We need meaningful labor almost as much as we need food, water, and oxygen. To deprive anyone of this is not only a tragic mistake, but cruel. Our welfare system has done good in some cases, but overall it has been a tragic and cruel yoke of bondage on the very ones who deserve the most to be free.

> The only solid ground is the kingdom of God, and we must build our lives on the kingdom.

Entitlements have a huge number of people thinking that the government owes them, without doing one thing to earn it. Most of these have no skills to help themselves, and do not even know where to start. A lot of their rage is based in fear. Even our government, the wealthiest and most powerful in the world, cannot take too many Katrina level disasters without being reduced to just trying to keep order, and not having anything to give the people. There will be riots and lawlessness when this happens on a scale that few comprehend in every nation that has been built on the socialist mentality. If we do not work fast to reverse this, we will pay a most terrible price in the future.

THE RECIPE

What the church releases in heaven gets released on the earth as we are told in Matthew 16:17-20. The church is called to be the light of the world, and it will be. It will have the answers to the world's ultimate problems. However, before we can pull anyone else out of the quicksand we must be standing on solid ground. The only solid ground is the kingdom of God, and we must build our lives on the kingdom.

We, MorningStar, became engaged in the Katrina relief efforts because of a prophetic understanding that disaster relief is going to be an essential and powerful ministry of the church in the time to come. It will help the church reap a great harvest, but that is not the only reason why we must do this—we must love our neighbors. The Helper we have been given loves and wants to help all people, even if they reject Him. It is simply the right thing to do, and is a basic part of our commission in this world.

If we have built our lives on solid ground, the kingdom, then we must demonstrate the power of God's love for the world. He has redeemed the world, and we are here to start the process of reconciling the world to Him. This will lead to its restoration. In the beginning, the Spirit of God moved upon the chaos and brought forth this beautiful creation. He knows how to deal with chaos, and seems to even love using it to demonstrate what He can do. When we see a disaster or chaos in any form and we are walking in faith, we will have an expectation of seeing the Holy Spirit do great things. True warriors run to the sound of battle, not away from it. Those who are truly filled with the Spirit will respond to those crying "help" because the Spirit is the Helper.

> **The Helper we have been given loves and wants to help all people, even if they reject Him.**

If we will move forward in faith, becoming proactive in our communities, we will see great miracles and pluck many out of the fire. Our students and volunteers who spent just a week at our Katrina relief base received more out of that week that they had in many years just sitting in church. The impact was far greater in building our church, dispelling lukewarmness, and delivering Christians from their apathy than just about anything we have ever done.

Even so, as great as the church was in responding to Katrina, we can do much better. I do not want to just point at the government's or other large charities' mismanagement, but rather learn from it so that we can do better. We also need to understand how many churches have drifted into a form of socialism that is crippling our people and leading them to bondage, not the liberty of the Spirit.

A great mobilization is coming among Christians. A great unity will also come. The church is about to become a true representative of the most powerful government there is—the kingdom of God, which is coming. It is time to prepare the way for the Lord. ∎

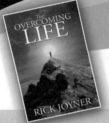

THE NEHEMIAH PROJECT

PROPHESY TO THE MANY WHO WILL STAY IN YOUR ROOM.

You, your family, church, business, or group can restore a hotel room at H.I.M. Each room you help to restore will be named in your honor or as a memorial to the one you choose.

JOIN THE PROJECT. SPONSOR A ROOM. ARISE & BUILD.

For more information, call 1-800-542-0278, visit us online at HIM.MorningStarMinistries.org, or write to 375 Star Light Drive, Fort Mill, SC 29715.

MFM Directory

The MorningStar Fellowship of Ministries

The MorningStar Fellowship of Ministries (MFM) was founded to serve three basic parts of the overall vision of MorningStar. First is the equipping, oversight, and support of ministries related to MorningStar. The second is to use the relationship that MorningStar has with many different parts of the body of Christ to promote interchange, understanding, and friendship between them. The third is for the mobilization of spiritual forces for the sake of the gospel. Current members of MFM are listed below. For more information or an application, please call our office at (803) 802-5544 ext. 247.

CANADA

Dean Downey (Pastor)
Vineyard House X—Montreal
119 Rene Emard, Ile Perrot,
Quebec J7V 8V5, CANADA
(514) 425-0523 / E-mail: come2vhx@yahoo.ca

Sylvain Gauthier
Najoth Ministries
784 Rang 7, Ste-Clothilde Beauce
Quebec G0N 1C0, CANADA
(418) 484-5611 / Fax: (418) 484-6611
E-mail: najoth@globetrotter.net

Nelson Richardson
Maranatha Fellowship
4 James Long Court,
Nepean, Ottawa, Ontario CANADA   K2J4R1
(613) 823-6815

Bryan Yager
Eagleview Ministries
205 Meadowbrook Road,
Victoria, British Columbia V9E 1J5, CANADA
(250) 479-7166 / Fax: (250) 479-7168
E-mail: Rolem@shaw.ca

OTHER COUNTRIES

Dr. Francis Agbana (Pastor)
Life Builders International Network
P.O. Box 23808, London SE, 15 1ZL England,
UK and P.O. Box 307, Lome Republic of Togo,
WEST AFRICA
E-mail: nationsowner@yahoo.com

Aivars Alksnis (Pastor)
Sigulda City Evangelical Church of Christ
Krasotaju iela 21-16, Riga, Latvia LV—1009
+371 959 1321 / Fax: +371 714 1008
E-mail: revival.ms@inbox.lv

Rod & Kerrie Christensen
Rivers of Living Water Inc.
21 Heathfield Dve Landsdale
Perth, Western Australia 6065
0011-618-9302-2305 / Fax: 0011-618-9302-2305
Rivliv@bigpond.net.au / www.riversliving.com

K.V. Daniel
Voice of Gospel
Voice of Gospel Worship Center
91-487-2-444301; Fax: 91-487-2-440683
E-mail: pastordaniel@rediftmail.com
www.voice of gospelministry.org
Kerala, INDIA

David Daynes
Worship Leader and Elder Downs Baptist Church
PO Box 70 Woodingdean
Brighton, England, BN2 6XZ
+ 44 1273 691802
E-mail: office@downsbaptistchurch.org
www.downsbaptistchurch.org

Nanette Diogo
Light on the Word
858 3rd Ave. PMB #451, Chula Vista, CA 91911
Voice Mail: (619) 540-7590
E-mail: mndiogo@prodigy.net.mx

George Ferrar
Tree of Life Ministries
2026 Arrowhead Drive, Traverse City, MI 49686
(231) 946-5622
E-mail: gferrar@btl.net / www.treeoflifebelize.com

Marvin D. Fisher (Pastor)
Genesis Ministries—Romania
Marasesti 2, Brasov Romania 500046
+ 40745319429
E-mail: mdfisher@genesisministry.org
www.genesisministry.org

Conrad Gille
Face to Face
Auf dem Weiler 2, Bonn, NRW 53175, Germany
E-mail: Conrad@fatofa.org / www.fatofa.org

Richard & Audrey Ho
Streams Revival Ministries
658h 27/154 Taman Bukit Anggerik
Cheras, Kuala Lumpur 56000, Malaysia
603-79806843 / E-mail: revival@tm.net.my

MFM Directory

Uli Hoyer
Hope Ministries E.V.
Gutzkowstr.79, D-60594 Frankfurt, Germany
+49 69 / 62 85 85
E-mail: uli.hoyer@hope-ministries.de
www.hope-ministries.de

Pieter Jordaan
Gateway Ministries
18 Mount Street, Aylesbury, Buckinghamshire
HP 20 2SE United Kingdom
+44 1296422669
E-mail: pieter@gatewayministry.org.uk
www.gatewayministry.org.uk

Andreas Keller (Pastor)
Stiftung Schleife
Pflanzschulstrasse 17, Postfach75, CH-8411
Winterthur, SWITZERLAND
+ 41 (52) 233-6080 / Fax: +41 (52) 233-6082
E-mail: office@schleife.ch / www.schleife.ch

Jerry McNally (Pastor)
Living Hope International
PO Box 116, West Bend, WI 53095-0116
(262) 364-2153
E-mail: Jerrymcnally@thecityofhope.org
www.thecityofhope.org / www.naciones.org.mx
www.lacuidaddeesperanza.org

Tommie Naumann
PO Box 60438, Thermi/Thessaloniki, Greece
+30-2310-805990
E-mail: tnaumannotenet.gr

Michael Quinn
Resurrection Life Ministries
A/K 542, LV-1050 Riga, Latvia
+ 371-883-6279 / E-mail: RlifeMin@aol.com

Ray Robertson (Pastor)
Genesis Ministries—Romania
Marasesti No 2, Brasov, Romania 500046
+40 0745130334
E-mail: rayrobertson@genesisministry.org
www.genesisministry.org

Ferry Wieland (Pastor)
Christian Fellowship Drachten
Torenstraat 18, Drachten 9203 BG Netherlands
+31 (51) 234-1095 / E-mail: cfd@hiscfd.com
www.hiscfd.com

UNITED STATES

ALABAMA

Miles Wylie Albright (Pastor)
Day's Dawn Ministries
245 C.R. 1595, Baileyton, AL 35019
(256) 796-2333

Ernest E. Brown (Pastor)
The Christian Center
9105 Alabama Hwy 69, Arab, AL 35016
(256) 753-2237 / Fax: (256) 582-9889
E-mail: erniebrown@juno.com
www.thechristiancenter.us

Charles Payne, Jr. (Pastor)
Open Door Fellowship
722 Scenic Drive NE, Cullman, AL 35055
(256) 682-2645 / E-mail: CPayne3004@aol.com

Tracy Schellhorn
Manifest Ministries International
PO Box 382227, Birmingham, AL 35238
(205) 980-4996
E-mail: mmitoday@bellsouth.net
www.manifestministries.com

ARIZONA

Cory McClure (Pastor)
LifeWay Christian Fellowship
1440 S. Country Club Drive #12, Mesa, AZ 85210
(480) 892-4522
E-mail: office@lifewayfellowship.org
www.lifewayfellowship.org

ARKANSAS

Randy & Crystal Moser (Pastor)
The Gatherings
87 Nieboer Drive, Mountain Home, AR 72653
(870) 491-5299 / Fax: (870) 491-5353
E-mail: moserbunch@centurytel.net
www.gatheringmtnhome.com

CALIFORNIA

Kim & Mary Andersson (Pastor)
Christ the Rock Fellowship
PO Box 1747, Anderson, CA 96007
(530) 365-5048 / www.christ-the-rock.org

Josh Dehmlow (Pastor)
Living Stones
PO box 4244, Fresno, CA 93704
(559) 444-0933
E-mail: livingstonescf@comcast.net
www.Livingstonescf.org

Harold D. Hanselman
House of Restoration
PO Box 142, Joshua Tree, CA 92252
(760) 366-2147
E-mail: Restoration@nethere.com

MFM Directory

CONNECTICUT

Craig and Amy Bassett
Atlantic Missionary Aviation Inc.
70 Rubbie Road, Tolland, CT 06084
(860) 559-9228
E-mail: craig.bassett@altlanticmissionav.org
www.atlanticmissionav.org

Weston Brooks (Pastor)
River of Life Christian Fellowship
384 Merrow Road, Tolland, CT 06084
Phone: (860) 871-1070
E-mail: pastor@rolcf.net / www.rolcf.net

Dan Evans (Pastor)
Mount Zion Christian Fellowship
PO Box 9215, 104 Notch Road
Bolton, CT 06043
(860)-643-8083 / Fax: (860) 649-5921

Chris Fields
NE Women in Ministry
449 So. River Road, Tolland, CT 06084
(860) 906-7580 / Fax (860) 871-1705
E-mail: chrisfields@snet.net
www.newomeninministry.org

Russell Leitch
Spirit Builders
16 Glenview Drive, Cromwell, CT 06416
Phone/Fax: (860) 635-2910
E-mail: spiritbuilders@juno.com

Rick McKinnis(Pastor)
Wellspring
222 Lincoln Steet, Kensington, CT 06037
Phone/Fax: (860) 225-0661
E-mail: spiritbuilders@juno.com

DISTRICT OF COLUMBIA

Wade Taylor
PO Box 15292, Washington, D.C. 20003
(202) 365-1685 / E-mail: wetbanner@aol.com
www.wadetaylor.org

FLORIDA

Gerrick and Jill Busl
Sabbath House Ministries
2720 SE Kern Rd., Port Saint Lucie, FL 34984
(772) 340-5807 / Fax: (772) 340-7328
E-mail: gerrickbusl@yahoo.com
jillbusl@netscape.net

Emmett Cooper
HoneyWord
PO Box 939, San Antonio, FL 33576
(352) 518-0189 / Fax: (352) 518-0707
E-mail: HoneyWord@aol.com
www.HoneyWord.com

Randal Cutter (Pastor)
New Dawn Community Church
11030 Wiles Road, Coral Springs, FL 33076
(954) 753-7729 / Fax: (954) 345-2562
E-mail: NewDawn@NewDawn.org
www.newdawn.org

Andrew DeLong (Pastor)
Tree of Life Church
2132 Shadowlawn Drive, Naples, FL 34112
(239) 530-2200 / Fax: (239) 530-2203
E-mail: Andrew@tlcnaples.org
www.tlcnaples.org

Lucy Finch
451 Bayfront Place #5311, Naples, FL 34102
E-mail: LucyPull@aol.com

David Hartz (Pastor)
Cherith Ministry/The Gathering
2304 Cobb Drive, Tallahassee, FL 32312
(850) 893-3032 / Fax: (850) 893-0658
E-mail: davidh248@hotmail.com
www.aboutthegathering.com

Rick Irving
Kingdom First Ministries
45 Ohio Blvd., Eustis, FL 32726
Phone/Fax: (352) 357-5700
E-mail: Rick@thekingdomfirst.com
www.thekingdomfirst.com

John David & Sarah Kirby
John David Kirby Ministries, Inc
4690 Woodstock Road, St. James City, FL 33956
(239) 283-2553
eagleprophet@earthlink.net /
www.jkdministries.com

Jean LaCour
NET Training Institute
PO Box 536875, Orlando, FL 32853
(407) 236-9400 / Fax: (407) 849-1120
E-mail: nti@netinstitute.net
www.netinstitute.net

Gene Paul & Debra J. Nesgoda
Front Line Word Ministries, Inc.
803 South Lois Avenue, Tampa, FL 33609
(813) 286-0929 / Fax: (813) 286-9798
E-mail: genepaulbldg@msn.com
songofdebra@msn.com

Reggie & Gina Parker (Pastors)
Mighty Warriors Prophetic Ministries
1333 Don Carlos Trail, Deltona, FL 32725
(386) 575-2855
E-mail: mwmmin@bellsouth.net

John Powell (Pastor)
Narrow Way Ministries
1301-Suite 17 Monument Road
Jacksonville, FL 32225
(904) 721-9963 / E-mail: jpowell133@aol.com

MFM Directory

Greg Pusateri (Pastor)
Grace Community Fellowship
P.O. Box 1072, Starke, FL 32091
(904) 964-7208 / E-mail: gracecf@atlantic.net
www.gracecommunityfellowship.com

Linda Spaulding
Levite Ministry
1224 Maple Street, Lakeland, FL 33810
(863) 858-5883
E-mail: Linda@leviteministry.com
www.leviteministry.com

Keith Upchurch (Pastor)
Liberty Ministries and Fellowship:
God's House Church
210 N. Lakeshore Way, Lake Alfred, FL 33850
Mailing Address: P.O. Box 9174,
Winter Haven, FL 23883
(863) 299-7936 / E-mail: klupchurch@juno.com

Craig Wendel (Pastor)
Tree of Life Church
2132 Shadowlawn Drive, Naples, FL 34112
(239) 530-2200 / Fax: (239) 530-2203
E-mail: Craig@TLCNAPLES.org
www.TLCNAPLES.org

GEORGIA

Jeff Carter
The Four Streams
1922 Chase Common Court, Norcross, GA 30071
(770) 368-1679 / www.thefourstreams.com

Craig Cooper
Relationship Church
1745 Houston Valley Rd., Ringgold, GA 30736
(706) 259-7677
E-mail: ccooper@relationshipchurch.com
www.relationshipchurch.com

Mike & Becky Chaille
Firestarter Ministries International
7523 Ridge Road, Hiram, GA 30141
(770) 439-2397 / Fax (770) 949-9702
E-mail: mike@chaille.us;becky@chaille.us
www.firestarterminstries.org

Mike & Becky Chaille
Great Commission Fellowship
578 Brownsville Road
Powder Springs, GA 30127
(770) 949-8877 / Fax (770) 949-9702
E-mail: mike@gcfatlanta.org; or
becky@gcfatlanta.org / www.gcfatlanta.org

Johnny Enlow (Pastor)
Daystar International Christian Fellowship
4200 Perimeter Park South, Suite 103
Atlanta, GA 30341
(770) 452-7113
E-mail: elizabeth@daystaratlanta.org or
johnny@daystaratlanta.org
www.daystaratlanta.org

Bryan Gabriel (Pastor)
Integrity Fellowship Church
1015 Cherokee Road, Winterville, GA 30683
(706) 742-5732
E-mail: bmgabriel41@hotmail.com

Brian Hayes (Pastor)
The Gate Community Church (Formerly ICF)
Fayetteville, GA 30214
E-mail: hayes3dbd@yahoo.com

Ray Kiertekles
Restoration Life Ministries
4989 Peachtree Parkway, Norcross, GA 30092
(678) 485-7955 / E-mail: RLMRSK@aol.com

Marc Lawson (Pastor)
Church at North Gate
9876 Main Steet, Suite 250
Woodstock, GA 30188
(678) 494-2193 / E-mail: info@ngca.org
www.NGCA.org

Ryan Lawson (Pastor)
Church at North Gate
P.O. Box 2190, Woodstock, GA 30188
(678) 494-2193 / E-mail: rlawson@NGCA.org
www.ngca.org

Keith Smith (Pastor)
Keith Smith Ministries, Inc.
9 South Bogey Drive, Jesup, GA 31546
(912) 427-6863
E-mail: elderkeithsmith@hotmail.com
www.providenceoutreachministries.org

HAWAII

Karen Nicoli
Good News Fellowship Ministries
140 Uwapo Road, #28203, Kihei, HI 96753
(808) 874-3652 / E-mail: Kearny777@yahoo.com

IDAHO

David McClellan (Pastor)
Strong Tower Ministries
4698 N. Tattenham Way, Boise, ID 83713
(208) 939-5155 / E-mail: davevicmc@msn.com

MFM Directory

ILLINOIS

Jason Black
Magdalene Society
2309 Delmar, Granite City, IL 62040
(618) 876-5497 / E-mail: jasonmblack@msn.com

Tony Danhelka
Riverwoods Christian Center
35 W 701 Riverwoods Lane
St Charles, IL 60174
(630) 263-2222, ext. 207 / Fax: (630) 443-0286
E-mail: tonydanhelka@sbcglobal.net
www.riverwoodschristiancenter.org
www.foxvalleycityreaching.org

Theresa Frerichs (Pastor)
Praise Ministries Church & Ministry Training Center
329 Stevens Street, Geneva, IL 60134
(630) 208-7818
E-mail: praiseminister@aol.com

Janice Fennell
4507 E. Rome Road, Chillicothe, IL 61523
(309) 274-5421 / Fax: (309) 274-4686
E-mail: janf@cmcousa.com
www.cmcousa.com / www.pritchardbrown.com

Georganne Schweickert
Knowing Him Ministries
21760 W. Washington Street, Grayslake, IL 60030

Hilton Thomas
3377 Maple Tree Lane, Wadsworth, IL 60083
(847) 858-3136 / Fax: (847) 244-1446
E-mail: Hilton.Thomas@att.net

Robert Whitt (Pastor)
Family Life Church
270 E. Chicago St., Elgin, IL 60120
(847) 717-4878 / Fax: (847) 697-4987
E-mail: familylifechurch1@ameritech.net
www.familylifechurch.com

INDIANA

Bob Combs
Let's Pray Ministries
3605 Poinsettia Drive, Indianapolis, IN 46227
(317) 881-1949
E-mail: letspray@es4mail.com

Doug Kimball
P.O. Box 473, Galveston, IN 46932
(317) 538-9216 / Fax: (574) 699-6184
E-mail: dougandkay@verizon.net
www.diamondsofpurpose.org

Michael Lee (Pastor)
The Prayer & Training Center
1901 Mansfield Street, Indianapolis, IN 46202
(317) 632-0206
E-mail: alee5@indy.rr.com
www.diamondsofpurpose.org

Betty K. Phillips
402 So. Fort Wayne Ave., Eaton, IN 47338
(765) 396-2089
E-mail: abagirL765@sbcglobal.net

John Andrew Sanders
Hobart Assembly of God
7545 East Ridge Rd., Hobart IN 46342
(219) 942-2691
E-mail: andycathy7@yahoo.com
www.andycathysanders.com

H. Dean Wollard (Pastor)
Cornerstone World Outreach Ministries
900 Huron Way, Auburn, IN 46706
(260) 925-4360

IOWA

David W. Brown
Eternity Project
150 W. Cedar St. / P.O. Box 76
Birmingham, IA 52535
(319) 498-4330
Email: Dbrown38@hotmail.com

Mike & Linda Schreurs
Intimacy with God Ministries
6829 River Bend Drive, Johnston, IA 50131
(515) 270-0231
E-mail: LMSCHREURS@aol.com
www.intimacy-with-God.com

KANSAS

Nick A. Harris (Pastor)
Living Waters House of Prayer
11441 E. Central, Wichita, KS 67206
(316) 686-9233 / Fax: (316) 686-8706
E-mail: livingwatershop@sbcglobal.net
www.livingwatershop.org

Jerry & Ruth Wickline (Pastors)
Spirit Life Church &
Schools of the Spirit Church Plants
11441 E. Central, Wichita, KS 67206
(620) 245-1058
E-mail: wicklines@cox.net
www.spiritlifeministries.net

MFM Directory

KENTUCKY

Alan & Anne Cash (Pastoral Elders)
Cornerstone Community Church
4465 Hansen Road, Paducah, KY 42001
(270) 554-9720 / Fax (270) 554-9723
E-mail: alancash@bellsouth.net

Marion Fawns (Pastor)
Church of the Harvest
2450 Osborne Road, Mt. Sterling, KY 40353
Phone/Fax: (859) 498-7983
E-mail: pastor@churchoftheharvest.net

Russell Wagner
Omega Network
333 E. Park Drive, Huntington, IN 46750
(260) 388-1130
www.omeganetworkonline.org

Tommy Hays
Messiah Ministries
2800 Tates Creek Road, Lexington, KY 40502
(859) 422-1794 / E-mail: messiahmin@aol.com
www.messiah-ministries.org

Sandy Lee
Walking In Destiny Ministries, Inc.
101 Geraldine Drive, Paducah, KY 42003
(270) 898-2626
E-mail: LeesDestiny@hotmail.com

LOUISIANA

Meg Jones
1938 Ferndale Avenue, Baton Rouge, LA 70808
(225) 383-5820 / E-mail: Rosedoor@aol.com

Denise LaPorte
The Spirit of the Nazarite
689 Apache Drive, Lake Charles, LA 70611
(337) 855-4827
E-mail: dmlappleeye@msn.com

LaRue Nance
Bethany Ministries and Nurture Int'l
5305 North Blvd, Alexandria, LA 71301
(409) 201-2001 / Fax: (318) 445-5653
E-mail: laruenance@aol.com
www.nurtureinternational.com

MAINE

John Connor
16 Summer Street, Winthrop, ME 04364
(207) 377-2015 / E-mail: jwconnor@ctel.net

Roy Roden (Pastor)
Prophetic Destiny Ministries
P.O. Box 711, Camden, Maine 04843
(207) 236-4904; / E-mail: destiny1@adelphia.net
www.propheticdestinyministries.org

MARYLAND

Brian Eichelberger
14308 Mount Oak Rd, Mitchellville, MD 20721
(301) 218-8380 / E-mail: bke5@verizon.net

John Metcalfe
4605 Olden Court, Bowie, MD 20715
(301) 262-6738 / E-mail: jmet_2000@yahoo.com

MASSACHUSETTS

Tom Dobrient
7 Oak Hill Road, Hyannis, MA 02601
(508) 776-8892 / Fax: (508) 778-6564
E-mail: Dobrient@cape.com

Barry Grauman (Pastor)
Taconic Valley Christian Fellowship
3399 Hancock Road, Williamstown, MA 01267
(413) 738-5814 / E-mail: TaconicVCF@aol.com
www.taconicvcf.org

Donna Milham
Eagle & Dove Ministries
P.O. Box 7094, Gloucester, MA 01930
(978) 283-9076 / E-mail: eagledove@adelphia.net
www.eagledove.com

MICHIGAN

Edward J. Kurdziel (Pastor)
Pure Heart Ministries
2020 Raybrook SE, Suite 101
Grand Rapids, MI 49546
(616) 464-5667; Fax: (616) 464-5688
E-mail: PUREHEARTCHURCH@sbcglobal.net
www.pureheartminstries.info

Kathy Ann Wuopio (Chaplain)
K & K D.A.Y.S.
PO Box 59, Clawson, MI 48017
E-mail: chapkathyann@hotmail.com
www.kandkdays.com

MINNESOTA

Pete & Pam Thiel
Firestarters Worship Center
PO Box 63, Ottertail, Minnesota 56571
(218) 367-3435
E-mail: contactus@firestartersmusic.com
www.firestartersmusic.com

MFM Directory

MISSOURI

David Apel
1809 County Road 1310, Moberly, MO 65270
(660) 263-0728 / E-mail: dave@newshiloh.net
www.newshiloh.net

Jack Keith Glasson
Seed Time Harvest
1729 County Road 1520, Moberly, MO 65270
(660) 263-1157 / E-mail: jacmon@socket.net

MONTANA

Tom C. Banks (Pastor)
International Church of Helena
609 S. Harris, Helena, MT 59601
(406) 439-6938
E-mail: ptbanks@juno.com

Albert LaRance (Pastor)
Morning Star House of Prayer
P.O. Box 1420, Lame Deer, MT 59043
(406) 477-6612 / Fax: (406) 477-6635
E-mail: getncontact@mshopchurch.org
www.morningstarhouseofprayer.org

Lloyd C. Phillips (Pastor)
FLINT Net (Fellow Laborers' Intl. Network)
P.O. Box 113, Missoula, MT 59806
(406) 251-8580 / Fax: (406) 251-7035
E-mail: flintnet@flintnet.org / www.flintnet.org

John & Sharon Senin
Fellowships Aflame
P.O. Box 2833, Kalispell, MT 59903
(406) 261-4323
E-mail: john0011@centurytel.net

NEBRASKA

Eric & Kristy Murray (Pastors)
Awake Ministries & The Dwelling Place Church
201 Hillcrest Ave., Bellevue, NE 68005
(402) 291-3353 / Fax: (402) 991-4819
E-mail: ericgmurray@yahoo.com
kristymurray@cox.net
www.thedwellingplacechurch.com

NEW HAMPSHIRE

Aaron Evans
Streams Ministries Intl.
P.O. Box 591, New London, NH 03257
(603) 995-6137 / (603) 927-4883
E-mail: sentbyhim@aol.com
www.stirthewater.com

NEW JERSEY

Ken Bellan
105 Chestnut Hill Lane, Columbus, NJ 08085
(856) 467-0986 / E-mail: KGBellan@juno.com

Steve Burton (Pastor)
House of Praise Ministries
488 Monroeville Road, Woolwich, NJ 08085
(856) 467-0986
E-mail: Freedom8800@yahoo.com

Margaret Clark (Pastor)
The Gospel Fellowship
626 Plainsboro Road, Plainsboro, NJ 08536
(609) 799-5637 / Fax: (609) 799-0012
E-mail: gfcommunicate@earthlink.com

Dan McKeon (Pastor)
LifeSpring Church
P.O. Box 11247, Yardville, NJ 08020
(609) 387-4230 / Fax: (609) 387-4230
E-mail: LifeSpringChurch@aol.com
Meets at: Lakeside Community Center
Lakeside Blvd, Hamilton, NJ 08610

David & Evelyn Scull (Pastors)
Jubilee Living Word Ministries
62 Gravely Hill Road, PO Box 333
Quinton, NJ 08072-0333
(856) 451-1356 / Fax: (856) 451-2288
E-mail: david_scull@comcast.net

Andrew Surace (Pastor)
Covenant Life Christian Fellowship
PO Box 1038, Marmora, NJ 08223
(609) 390-1999 / Fax: (609) 390-7445
E-mail: Drew5Aces@aol.com
www.covenantlifenj.com

NEW MEXICO

Bonita Eichorst
Whole Ministries
1309 Los Griegos Rd
Jemez Springs, NM 87025
(505) 829-4524
Email: whole@wholeministries.org
www.wholeministries.org

NEW YORK

Joanie Boring
4856 Hitchcock Road, Odessa, NY 14869
(607) 594-2293
Email: michael1@empireaccess.net

Dylan Bowden (Pastor)
New Covenant Community Church
86 Broad St., Schuylerville, NY 12871
(518) 695-5534/ Fax (518) 675-5655
www.newcovenantcommunity.org

Gail Breden
The Word & Spirit Ministries
P.O. Box 445, Walden, NY 12586
(845) 778-7086 / E-mail: Gail_B@juno.com
www.WordandSpiritMinistries.com

Bob & Kathy Campbell (Pastors)
Harvest International Family Church
4647 Reservoir Road, Geneseo, NY 14454
Phone/Fax: (585) 243-9280
E-mail: HFNC@FLMTGIF.org
www.HIFC.org

Diane M. Czekala
Restore the Glory Ministries
435 Main St. Johnson City, NY 13790
(607) 729-7500
E-mail: MDCZekala@yahoo.com
Website: www.healingbinghamton.com

Roy & Marie Esposito (Pastor)
Restoration Christian Fellowship
P.O. Box 1194, East Northport, NY 11731
(631) 651-9689 / www.rcf-church.org

James Exner (Pastor)
Syracuse Airport Christian Fellowship/Ministries
7744 Frontage Road Plaza, Cicero, NY 13039
(315) 458-4210 / Fax: (315) 699-9329
www.RC7-church.org

Dan Farley
Public Square Ministries, Inc
2725 Grandview Pl., Endwell, NY 13760
(607) 754-6355 / E-mail: dfarley@stny.rr.com
www.PSministries.org

Fred & Donna Hoover (Pastors)
Abide in the Vine Fellowship
1018 Lillie Hill Road, Appalachin, NY 13732
(607) 625-5907 / Fax: (607) 689-0043
E-mail: fhoover@stny.rr.com

Tom & Marianne Kapinos
Fellowship of the Cross
2743A South Park Ave., Lackawanna, NY 14218
Bus: (716) 912-8580 / Fax: (716) 824-7676
E-mail: mannonthecross@aol.com

Jim & Peg McLaughlin (Pastors)
New Beginnings Church
15 Silver St., Norwich, NY 13815
Phone (607) 334-2833 / Fax:: (607) 334-3860
E-mail: jrmclaughlin@juno.com
www.nbcnorwich.org

Paul Pomeroy
Public Square Ministries
146 Dyer Flat Rd, Ninevah, NY 13813
(607) 693-3305
Email: Paulandterry26@aol.com

Diane Scalchunes (Pastor)
Deep Waters Ministry
P.O. Box 2091, Port Washington, NY 11050
E-mail: deepwaters@optonline.net
www.deepwatersministry.com

Robert Seymour (Pastor)
Abide in the Vine Fellowship
1277 Taylor Road, Owego, NY 13827
(607) 642-9944 / Fax: (607) 687-0043
E-mail: besttoots@pronetisp.net

NORTH CAROLINA

Jothi Ambrose
Apostolic Prophetic Destiny
9005 Cinder Lane, Huntersville, NC 28078
(704) 992-1348
E-mail: jothiambrose@hotmail.com

Bill & Karen Baldwin
Truth to the Nations
PO Box 202, Albemarle, NC 28002
(704) 986-4056/ Fax (704) 983-2408
E-mail: tttn@ctc.net / www.truthtothenations.com

Sally Boenau
122 S. Greenbriar Woods Rd
Hendersonville, NC 28739
(828) 697-2172 / E-mail: bripatch@brinet.com

Jeff and Jacqueline Chappell
13607 Christian Tyler Ct., Charlotte, NC 28278
(704)986-4056 / E-mail: plsticsman@christfirst.net

Bruce & Krista Corwin
Trinity Christian Prep School
6411 Sharon Road, Charlotte, NC 28210
(704) 554-0092 / Fax: (704) 552-6299
E-mail: btc@trinityprep.com
www.trinityprep.com

Emmett Cooper
HoneyWord
251 Heritage Blvd., Fort Mill, SC 29715
E-mail: HoneyWord@aol.com
Website: www.HoneyWord.com

Earl & Sabrina Coulston
Accounts Ministry
P.O. Box 174, Pineville, NC 28134
(704) 543-7143 / Fax: (704) 544-2729
E-mail: Acoulston@aol.com

MFM Directory

Maggie Deller
MorningStar Fellowship Church
375 Star Light Drive, Fort Mill, SC 29715
(803) 802-5544 / www.morningstarministries.org

Trisha Doran
MorningStar Fellowship Church
375 Star Light Drive, Fort Mill, SC 29715
(803) 802-5544 / www.morningstarministries.org

Tom Elkins (Pastor)
1017 South Croadway St., Forest City, NC 28043
(828) 245-7766

Marla Filotei
Power in the Word Ministries, Int.
1326 Pearl Crescent Drive, Charlotte, NC 28216
(704) 392-2027
E-mail: Ephesians6@aol.com

John Hansen
MorningStar Fellowship Church
375 Star Light Drive, Fort Mill, SC 29715
(803) 802-5544 / www.morningstarministries.org

Tom Hardiman (Pastor)
MorningStar Fellowship Church
375 Star Light Drive, Fort Mill, SC 29715
(803) 802-5544 / www.morningstarministries.org

David Hart
MorningStar Fellowship Church
375 Star Light Drive, Fort Mill, SC 29715
(803) 802-5544 / www.morningstarministries.org

Carroll Henderson Jr. (Pastor)
Laurel Wood Ministries
403 West Maryland Ave.
Bessemer City, NC 28016
Phone: (704) 629-0456 / Fax: (704) 629-0262
E-mail: jrscch@bellsouth.net

Jim Hill
His Heart Missions
P.O. Box 1742, Mooresville, NC 28115
E-mail: hisheartmissions@aol.com

Reggie & Debbie Hill
Helping Hands, Inc.
1241 Briar Creed Road, Charlotte, NC 28205
Phone / Fax: (704) 568-7905
E-mail: 1way2him@helpinghandsinc.org

John Holcomb
MorningStar Fellowship Church
375 Star Light Drive, Fort Mill, SC 29715
(803) 802-5544 / www.morningstarministries.org

Terry Howell (Pastor)
Evangel Fellowship
724 Oakland Road, Spindale, NC 28160
(828)-287-2868 / Fax: (828) 287-3170
E-mail: Thowell123@charter.net

Bobby & Ginger Hussey (Pastors)
MorningStar Fellowship Church
375 Star Light Drive, Fort Mill, SC 29715
(803) 802-5544 / www.morningstarministries.org

Leonard Jones
MorningStar Fellowship Church
375 Star Light Drive, Fort Mill, SC 29715
(803) 802-5544 / www.morningstarministries.org

Rick Joyner (Senior Pastor)
MorningStar Fellowship Church
375 Star Light Drive, Fort Mill, SC 29715
(803) 802-5544 / www.morningstarministries.org

Dean Kaneshiro
MorningStar Fellowship Church
375 Star Light Drive, Fort Mill, SC 29715
(803) 802-5544 / www.morningstarministries.org

Joel Killion (Teacher)
Inner Life Ministries
2511 Stedman Drive, Wilson, NC 27896
(252) 291-22946 / E-mail: joelkillion@yahoo.com
www.innerlife.injesus.com
www.cheribimnetwork.com

Steve Lappin (Pastor)
2014 Cardinal Loop, Stanley, NC 28164
(704) 822-2412 / Fax: (704) 822-2413
E-mail: steve@charlottebythelake.com
www.charlottebythelake.com

Steve Martin (Administrator)
Vision for Israel
P.O. Box 19501, Charlotte, NC 28219
(704) 357-3556 / Fax: (704) 357-1413
E-mail: stevemartin@dpmusa.org
www.dpmusa.org

Robin McMillan (Pastor)
MorningStar Fellowship Church
375 Star Light Drive, Fort Mill, SC 29715
(803) 802-5544 / www.morningstarministries.org

Brad McClendon (Pastor)
MorningStar Fellowship Church
375 Star Light Drive, Fort Mill, SC 29715
(803) 802-5544 / www.morningstarministries.org

Scott McClelland
11706 Five Cedars Road, Charlotte, NC 28226
(704) 340-2297 / E-mail: voiceof1@earthlink.net

Bill NeSmith
Harvest Light Ministries
11944 Harmon Lane, Pineville, NC 28134
E-mail: bill.nesmith@harvestLM.org
www.harvestlight.org

Travis Newton
7235 Wingstone Lane, Charlotte, NC 28262
(704) 503-1086 / E-mail: JTN555@aol.com

Jorge Parrott
Christ's Mandate for Missions
P.O. Box 7705, Charlotte, NC 28241
(704) 517-2557; Fax (888) 816-0725
E-mail: officecmm@gmail.com
www.cmmissions.net

Matt Peterson (Pastor)
MorningStar Fellowship Church
375 Star Light Drive, Fort Mill, SC 29715
(803) 802-5544 / www.morningstarministries.org

Nathan Plowman (Pastor)
MorningStar Fellowship Church
375 Star Light Drive, Fort Mill, SC 29715
(803) 802-5544 / www.morningstarministries.org

Jon & Freddie Powers
Keeping Hope Alive
10927 Carver Pond Road, Charlotte, NC 28269
Email: jdpfms@earthlink.net

Carey & Suzanne Ramsey
Lovingkindness Ministries
690 Sink Road, Lexington, NC 27295
Phone/Fax: (336) 224-1216
E-mail: careyram@lexcominc.net

Don Robertson
DREAM of Restoration Ministries
P.O. Box 300, Glendale Springs, NC 28629
(336) 982-3526 / Fax: (336) 982-3521
E-mail: phil211@skybest.com

Steven (Pastor) & Mindy Scroggs
Mountain Vintage Fellowship
3867 Sweeten Creek Road, Arden, NC 28704
(828) 687-9234 / Fax: (828) 687-0628
E-mail: community@mountainvintage.org
www.mountainvintage.org

Alan Smith
Stony Point Christian Publications
P.O. Box 231, Stony Point, NC 28678
(704) 585-2355 / Fax: (704) 585-2302
www.spchristianpub.org

Beverly Smith
Beverly Smith Ministries
2828 Queen City Drive, Suite H
Charlotte, NC 28208
(704) 398-7332 / Fax: (704) 398-7342
E-mail: bsmtruth@bellsouth.net
www.beverlysmithministries.org/www.wdcp.org

Rick Stoker
First Fruit Ministries
2750 Vance Street, Wilmington, NC 28412
(910) 612-9437 / Fax: (910) 452-0211
E-mail: rickstoker@bellsouth.net
www.firstfruitministries.org

Randy Strombeck
437 Hollywood Rd, Moravian Falls, NC 28654
(336) 838-6701 / Fax: (336) 838-6702
E-mail: rcdconstruction@riverco.net

Clifton Sutton (Pastor)
Just Like Jesus Ministries
P.O. Box 130, Burlington, NC 27215
(336) 538-1616 / Fax: (336) 584-0040
Email: cliftonsutton@bellsouth.net
www.justlikejesus.org

Steve Thompson (Pastor)
MorningStar Fellowship Church
375 Star Light Drive, Fort Mill, SC 29715
(803) 802-5544 / www.morningstarministries.org

Trevor Tiessen
MorningStar Fellowship Church
375 Star Light Drive, Fort Mill, SC 29715
(803) 802-5544 / www.morningstarministries.org

James and Rhonda Tomasi
International Christian Servants, Inc.
E-mail: jtomasi62@hotmail.com
www.icservants.org

Rev. Jeanne Turner
Light of the World Ministries
P.O. Box 744, Moravian Falls, NC 28654
(803) 429-8587 / E-mail: rohal&turner@wilkes.net

David White
Knights of the Cross MorningStar Ministries
375 Star Light Drive, Fort Mill, SC 29715
(336) 667-0359 / www.morningstarministries.org
E-mail: koc@morningstarministries.org

Robert & Kathy Whitlow
Providence Ventures
6700 Providence Road, Charlotte, NC 28226
E-mail: PROVVENINC@aol.com

MFM Directory

Byron Wicker (Pastor)
River Life Fellowship
2487 Charlotte Highway, Mooresville, NC 28117
(704) 664-3540 / Fax: (704) 799-1928
E-mail: Bulrushes@alltel.net
www.riverlifefellowship.org

Michael & Kathy Winfree
Bridge to the Nations Ministries
1374 Rock Crab Way, Shallotte, NC 28470
E-mail: bridgingtogether@aol.com

Al Woods
MorningStar Fellowship Church
375 Star Light Drive, Fort Mill, SC 29715
(803) 802-5544 / www.morningstarministries.org

Suzy Yaraei
MorningStar Fellowship Church
375 Star Light Drive, Fort Mill, SC 29715
(803) 802-5544 / www.morningstarministries.org

NORTH DAKOTA

Andrea Veach
301 7th Ave S.E., Rugby, ND 58368
(701) 776-5890 / E-mail: dveach@state.ND.US

OHIO

David Davenport
E-mail: mustpresson@aol.com

David & Donna Kelly (Pastors)
Passion and Fire Worship Center
P.O. Box 145, West Chester, OH 45071-0145
(513) 777-8217 / Fax: (513) 777-8209
E-mail: pfworshipcenter@aol.com
www.passionandfire.org

Hombre Liggett (Pastor)
Church of the Harvest
420 W. Third Street, Dover, OH 44622
(330) 343-1905
E-mail: contact@harvestchurch.com
www.harvestchurch.com

Timothy Martin (Pastor)
His Glorious Church
Meets at: St. Route 170, East Liverpool, OH 43920
Mailing Address: 540 Henry Ave.
East Liverpool, OH 43920
(330) 843-4895

David Mullikin
428 Maple Street, Sugarcreek, OH 44681
E-mail: warriorshepherd@juno.com

Barry & Tricia Tucker
519 Hazel Hurst St., New Lebanon, OH 45345
(937) 687-4340

Scott & Grace Veatch
6677 Dublin Road, Delaware, OH 43015
(614) 554-5073

OREGON

Robert Haaby (Pastor)
Eagle Mountain Fellowship
P21300 SE Bear Creek Road, Bend, OR 97701
Phone: (541) 312-9345
E-mail: emf@bendcable.com
www.eaglemountainfellowship.org

Ray & Kay Maestas (Pastors)
Harvest Rock Community Church
225 SW 1st Ave #8, Ontario, OR 97914
Phone: (541) 889-6625 / Fax: (541) 889-3915
E-mail: rgmaes@aol.com

James Moore
Salem House of Prayer
2037 Walker Road NE, Salem, OR 97301
Phone / Fax: (503) 585-7467
E-mail: salemhouseofprayer@yahoo.com

Jacob Ray
Life Church/ Zoe Kids
255 College Drive NW, Salem, OR 97304
(503) 362-0362 Fax: (503) 588-4348
E-mail: jakeilifeschool.com
www.ilifeschool.com

Mark & Sharon Stevens
Evening Light Ministries
3456 NE 145th Ave., Portland, OR 97230
(503) 252-3275
E-mail: Psmark@aol.com

Allen R. Tillford
Hearts for Humanity
2830 Arrowhead St., Eugene, OR 97404
(541) 688-0003
E-mail: allent@hearts4humanity.org
www.hearts4humanity.org

PENNSYLVANIA

David E. Barnett
New Song Community Church
6 Briarwood Ct., Mechanicsburg, PA 17050
(717) 796-1978 / E-mail: newsongcc@juno.com

Cynthia Brubaker (Pastor)

Glenside / Abington United Methodist Churches
412 E. Sentner Street, Philadelphia, PA 19120
(215) 535-4930 / E-mail: randy.cindy@juno.com

Gregory Buzzanco (Pastor)

Triumphant Life Church
5651 Perry Highway, Erie, PA 16509
(814) 864-3984 / Fax: (814) 465-3597
E-mail: Greg@triumphantlifechurch.com
www.triumphantlifechurch.com

Stanton R. & Nancy J. Higley (Pastors)

New Life Fellowship World Outreach Center
PO Box 22, 4326 Rte. 646, Cyclone, PA 16726
(814) 465-3272 / Fax: (814) 465-3597
E-mail: srnjhigley@hotmail.com

Matthew Buckwalter

P.O. Box 314, Gap, PA 17527
E-mail: judahezra@hotmail.com
(717) 333-6091

Ted Moyer (Pastor)

Rock Community Church
PO Box 64225, Souderton, PA 18964
(215) 723-8678
www.rockthechurch.org

Terry Smith (Pastor)

Jubilee Christian Center
20761 Shawville Croft Highway
Clearfield, PA 16830
(814) 765-1422
E-mail: jubilee888@pennswoods.net

Eugene Strite (Pastor)

World Harvest Outreach
1090 Wayne Ave., Chambersburg, PA 17201
(717) 709-1126
Email: whocenter@whocenter.org
www.whocenter.org

SOUTH CAROLINA

Jerry Ashley (Pastor)

Daystar Ministries
100 W. Richardson Avenue
Summerville, SC 29483
(843) 875-4370 / Fax: (843) 875-4341
E-mail: daystar@dycon.com

Terry Butler (Pastor)

New Covenant Praise Church
265 Wire Road, Aiken, SC 29801
(803) 648-7366 / Fax: (803) 648-9053
E-mail: tbutler265@msn.com
www.newcovenantpraise.org

Peggy Henderson Kannaday

Church Growth International
707 Torrey Pines Ln., Fort Mill, SC 29715
E-mail: socgikorea@yahoo.com
www.churchgrowthint.homestead.com/home.htm

Rodger Martin

616 Lakeview Boulevard, Hartsville, SC 29550
(843) 332-0468
E-mail: rodgerdmartin@juno.com

Bill Perry (Pastor)

Hartsville Community Fellowship
PO Box 1739, Hartsville, SC 29551
(843) 383-8555 / E-mail: HCF001@aol.com

Dr. Samuel Tyler

Vanguard Foursquare Church
650 West Blackstock Road
Spartanburg, SC 29301
Mailing Address: PO Box 170008
Spartanburg, SC 29301
(864) 574-2777 / Fax: (864) 574-0040
E-mail: vanguard@cfaith.com

TENNESSEE

Cris & Rebecca Bennett

B & B Ministries
(615) 599-2425 / Fax (877) 437-2594
E-mail: rythman@mail.com/ beccab@mail.com

Doug Floyd (Pastor)

Spring of Light
4426 Pinehurst Road, Louisville, TN 37777
(856) 983-9015
E-mail: doug@springoflight.org
www.springoflight.org

Scott MacLeod (Pastor)

Provision / Fortress Fellowship
1419 Clinton Street, Nashville, TN 37203
(615) 327-1200 / (615) 791-1181
E-mail: ScottMac7@lwol.com
www.provisioninternational.org
www.zadokministries.org

Mike McClung (Pastor)

Lionheart Fellowship / IHOP - Knoxville
1802 Airbase Road, Louisville, TN 37777
(865) 984-0302 / Fax: (865) 984-5809
E-mail: pastor@lionheartministries.org
www.lionheartministries.org

Thomas Patriss

Bridge of Promise Ministries
9775 Misty Bay Cove, Arlington, TN 38002
(901) 377-2241
E-mail: tpatriss2@midsouth.rr.com

Darrell Simbeck (Pastor)

Ascension Life Fellowship
1510 Nova Street, Athens, TN 37303
(423) 745-7290 / E-mail: Ascensionlife@aol.com

Susan Todd

Crossmember Ministries
32 Crossings Way #171, Crossville, TN 38555
(931) 200-2300
E-mail: crossmember@hotmail.com

MFM Directory

TEXAS

Scott Boyd
Fire and Ice Ministries
333 Bayberry Drive, Rockvall, TX 75087
(972) 22-7570
E-mail: Jsboyd76@yahoo.com
www.fairevival.com

Tara Dorroh
At His Feet Ministries
18351 Kuykendahl #463, Spring, TX 77379
(281) 320-9637 / Fax: (281) 251-2979
E-mail: athisfeet@pdq.net
www.athisfeetministries.org

David Fees (Pastor)
Christ Fellowship Ministries
P.O. Box 940326, Plano, TX 75094
(972) 423-2543
E-mail: dfees@cfminternational.org

Carl & Kristy Greer
2110 Bay Club, Arlington, TX 76013
(817) 261-7137 / Fax: (817) 274-2776
E-mail: coachcarl@comcast.net

Jeff Hooser
Advancing Truth Ministries
P.O. Box 540217, Grand Prairie, TX 75052-2554
(972) 262-4433
E-mail: jeff@advancingtruthministries.org,
www.advancingtruthministries.org

UTAH

Tracee Anne Loosle
Intrepid Heart Ministry
854 N. Dillon Drive, Ogden, Utah 84404
E-mail: traceeanne@intrepidheartministries.org
www.intrepidheartministries.org

VIRGINIA

Tony Eldridge (Pastor)
Warrior's Path International Ministries
13486 Glenbrook Ave. Meadowview, VA 27361
(276) 698-7247
E-mail: info@warriorspathinternational.org
www.warriorspathinternationa.org

Peggy Kannaday
411 23rd Street, Virginia Beach, VA 23451
(822) 783-3929 / Fax: (822) 784-1990
E-mail: peggy@uriel.net

WASHINGTON

Tom & Jackie Archer
25760 174th Place SE, Covington, WA 98042
(253) 638-8490 / E-mail: teamarchery@msn.com

Symon Boschma
Highway of Life Ministries
2007 Hampton Road, Everson, WA 98247
Phone/Fax: (360) 354-1395
E-mail: Symon@highstream.net

Ken & Deborah Deonigi
P.O. Box 1140, Maple Valley, WA 98038
(425) 413-9118 / E-mail: seajkd@covad.net
www.deonigi.com

Robert Foster (Pastor)
My Father's House Fellowship
Bellingham, WA 98226
(360) 202-4130
E-mail: Robert@mfhfellowship.org
www.mfhfellowship.org

Angela Greenig (Pastor)
Setfree Ministries International
428 8th St. SW #Warehouse 1 & 2
Auburn, WA 98003
(253) 863-8031 / E-mail: me@sfministries.org
www.sfministries.org

Lisa Kitchen
Aggressive Ministries
300 5th Ave. North, Algona, WA 98001
(253) 217-0119 / E-mail: Gapline1@aol.com

Paul "Red" & Patricia Wilson (Pastors)
Aggressive Ministries
P.O. Box 790, Sumner, WA 98390
(253) 279-5763 / Fax: (253) 862-1859
E-mail: aggressive@cfaith.com
www.aggressiveministries.org

WEST VIRGINIA

Demetrius Apostolon
Body of Christ Ministries
34 Hidden Valley Drive, Kenova WV 25530
(304) 453-5027 / Fax: (304) 453-5027
E-mail: apostolond@msn.com

WISCONSIN

Michael R. Gissibl
Freedom Ministries
N. 62 W. 27380 Trappers Run, Sussex, WI 53089
(414) 708-7063 / E-mail: mgissibl1@wi.rr.com